Creative Teaching

Also available from Continuum

Classroom Starters and Plenaries, Kate Brown

The Creative Teaching and Learning Toolkit, Brin Best and Will Thomas

The Creative Teaching and Learning Resource Book, Brin Best and Will Thomas

Letting the Buggers be Creative, Sue Cowley

Creative Teaching
Learning with Style

David Starbuck

A companion website to accompany this book is available
online at: http://education.starbuck.continuumbooks.com

Please type in the URL above and receive your unique
password for access to the book's online resources.

If you experience any problems accessing the resources,
please contact Continuum at: info@continuumbooks.com

continuum

Continuum International Publishing Group
The Tower Building   80 Maiden Lane
11 York Road   Suite 704
London SE1 7NX   New York NY 10038

www.continuumbooks.com

First edition published 2006

This revised edition published 2012

British Library Cataloguing-in-Publication Data
A catalogue record for this book is available from the British Library.

ISBN: 978-1-4411-1348-1 (paperback)
      978-1-4411-7591-5 (ePub)
      978-1-4411-0398-7 (PDF)

Library of Congress Cataloging-in-Publication Data
Starbuck, David.
    Creative teaching : learning with style / David Starbuck.
       p. cm.
Includes index.
ISBN 978-1-4411-1348-1 (pbk.) -- ISBN 978-1-4411-7591-5 (ebook)
(epub) -- ISBN 978-1-4411-0398-7 (ebook) (pdf)
1. Creative teaching. 2. Classroom environment. I. Title.

LB1044.88.S73 2012
371.102--dc23

                                                    2011036247

Typeset by Fakenham Prepress Solutions, Fakenham,
Norfolk NR21 8NN
Printed and bound in India

Contents

I have provided a selection of some of my favourite starters, middlers and enders that you might want to refer to when looking for some inspiration. You can find these on pages 98–123.

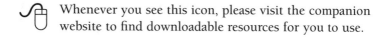 Whenever you see this icon, please visit the companion website to find downloadable resources for you to use.

Chapter One
Being creative

In this section:

1.1 Introduction: What is Creative Teaching?

'Pardon?' said the schoolteacher, his eyebrows arching like little horseshoes. 'You want me to like the buggers?'

'No,' said the slightly embattled education consultant, 'I merely suggest that you might like to give your pupils something other than lots of writing to do.'

'What?' the schoolteacher's rather large, heavy-looking moustache looked as if it was about to take off. 'What would be the point of that?!'

'Well, they might learn better and enjoy your subject more.' The education consultant, in her naturally optimistic manner smiled a tired smile.

'Good gracious, what would be the point of that?!' grunted the schoolteacher. As he marched down the corridor he chuckled and mused to himself, 'Imagine if pupils actually wanted to learn, how preposterous.' He entered his classroom, slammed the door behind him, and began ranting at his pupils about how lazy they were and how they did not take his subject seriously enough.

Creative teaching is when you appeal to the creative side of pupils' brains. If you would like to read some of the science behind creativity, I've explained it in the first Fact Box (pp. 00). Creative teaching can take many forms. Pupils may be in or out of their seats, they may be talking or working in silence, they may be working with you, in teams or by themselves. Creative teaching does not necessarily mean that you need to put in hours of preparation for every single activity you do, making up cards, activity packs and the like. This would in fact be a bad plan, as the pressure would remove any possibility of having a life outside of the classroom. While pupils might find it hard to believe that such a life exists, we teachers know that it does exist and that it is very precious to us!

The idea behind creative teaching is to enhance the learning process, and as such it should enhance your job too. It should be a satisfying and enjoyable experience for you as well as for your pupils. It's not selfish to want to enjoy your job.

Creative teaching is a mindset to enter into: consciously entering into what I call a *creative state*. It's about how you present yourself as someone who cares and enjoys teaching your subject; how you motivate your pupils to participate and understand; how you go about making learning more fun or engaging. It's about spotting opportunities to liven things up. It's about encouraging pupils to take responsibility for their work in a way that doesn't feel like a burden (to you or to the pupil).

It is very easy for a teacher to get into a protective, controlling mindset whereby every pupil's precise movement is contrived and dictated. In this kind of teaching pupils must do exactly as the teacher says, do the prescribed activities that are designed to keep them in their seats and stop them from talking to anyone. This method of teaching gives the teacher control, but it lacks right-brain creative input. Often it's used because class behaviour isn't very good and we feel that this is the only way to achieve any form of coherent structure for learning.

Creative teaching, done correctly, will move you beyond such comfort zones into areas of teaching that are far more rewarding for you and your pupils alike. It requires a certain amount of trust between you and them. This is not possible, of course, unless a clear and well-enforced discipline structure is in place first, otherwise chaos will ensue. Getting the conditions right first is the most important factor when teaching creatively.

FACT BOX – WHY TEACH CREATIVELY?

Actively noticing

Imagine that you've just bought a new car. You think it's an unusual car to have because you haven't seen too many of them about town. So why is it that when you drive your car out of the dealership, you notice at least half a dozen cars identical to your own?

Well, it's because your mind is 'actively noticing'. It sounds like a silly thing to say, but that is what it is doing. Pretty much at the hub of all your brain's activity is the *reticular activating system*, or RAS for short. It is the filter for all of your internal thoughts and for all the external information that comes through your senses. It's the bit of your brain that decides what you will and won't be conscious of. It tends to give priority to things that are new or surprising, and enables your mind to focus on things you find relevant or interesting. Hence the reason for being unable to stop yourself drifting off during a particularly long and boring lecture. Or finding it hard to concentrate when you're hungry or thirsty.

Logic and creativity

One way to ensure that a pupil's RAS doesn't filter you and your lessons out is to tap in to the different areas of their brains. We know that different sections of the brain are responsible for different tasks, and we know, broadly speaking, that the brain operates in two main ways: creatively and logically.

Although it is often said that your brain has two *halves* – a creative right half and a logical left half – this is purely figurative language. In reality, the creative and logical functions of your brain intermingle all over the place. But as it is quite convenient to talk about right-brain (creative) and left-brain (logical) functions then I shall use those terms.

Right-brain, creative, activities involve anything that taps into imagination, imagery, rhythm and rhyme. Whether you are running a guided imagery exercise, or getting the class to rap, draw sketches, or simply watch a good video, you are tapping into their right brains. Conversely anything that is text-based, or involves ordering and sequencing is left-brain. Solving simple maths puzzles, making a flow diagram and simply reading from the textbook are left-brain activities.

However, creativity is no good without order, and logic is not productive without an imaginative spark; so the two 'halves' need to form neural connections between each other to operate effectively and understand things fully. Tasks that use both sides of the brain stimulate neural connections and therefore tend to grab students' attention. Memory tends also to work best when the mind is engaged with the topic and the tasks. There are many ways to tap into the left–right mix, such as more complex or creative maths puzzles, teamwork, making association maps, or other diagrams that have an artistic element, drama sketches, role-play and creative writing. Later in this book we will look at preferred learning styles and multiple intelligences which also tap into the left–right brain mix.

Plenty of research tells us that a more creative approach to learning improves results. If pupils have an awareness of how they learn and an interest in the learning process, they take more care and have a greater control of their work. It gives them a sense of ownership over their work: it becomes personal. And we all know that as soon as you care about something personally, you focus better on it and perform better as a result. In terms of pupil learning, we'll call it improving their *learning performance*: their focus, energy, enthusiasm, comprehension and academic results.

The Campaign for Learning researches and promotes 'Learning to Learn' skills. They ran research projects in a range of schools around the UK between 2000 and 2010. Their research led them to conclude that there are seven key aspects to Learning to Learn and its successful implementation in the classroom (Campaign for Learning, 2010). The three core aspects are meta-cognition, that is to say reflective and strategic thinking; enquiry skills, which helps pupils to interact better with their learning; and a solid community in which learning is supported, shared and nurtured. These three areas are backed up by four further supporting aspects: good pedagogy that focuses on facilitating learning; tools that support learning and enquiry; personal responsibility from the learners (which CfL call learner action); and good CPD. Pupils and staff in the research schools were given a lot of training about how pupils learn and how they can manage their learning. These Learning to Learn pupils showed some remarkable development compared to other pupils not trained in these techniques. Teachers reported that their pupils were:

- much more adept at processing knowledge, taking the initiative and self-evaluating their learning performance

- more motivated, reflective and resourceful

- enjoying learning more than they had done and their self-confidence grew

- communicating and working with others better than before

- remembering and understanding what they were learning better than before

These are not anecdotal findings; these have been backed up by tests and comparisons that show an improvement in school results as well as ethos.

In order to have Learning to Learn pupils you also need Learning to Learn teachers working in a Learning to Learn school. Teachers need to involve and appear to value all their pupils, be a good role model and create a positive, motivating learning environment. Such an environment is *best* enabled by a school-wide approach to Learning to Learn, so that the same attitudes permeate the whole-school ethos and are not restricted to individual classrooms.

My company, Learning Performance, has been visiting schools since 1994 to train pupils and staff in Learning to Learn techniques. It has visited over half of all the UK's secondary schools offering regular input about how to make pupils aware of the learning process and empower them to take an interest in, and control over their learning. It is from the experiences gleaned from observations made in these schools that this book originally materialized. You see, a visit to a school gives a valuable snapshot of life in that school. What does it do to promote good learning habits? How happy and motivated are the teaching staff? How on-the-ball are the pupils? How much value is placed on keeping the building looking nice and creating displays that assist learning? How low or high are expectations of pupils and, for that matter, teachers?

But this book has not simply come about from observations made by outsiders. Since I worked on the first edition, I have been privileged enough to work in a fantastically forward-thinking and outstanding Learning to Learn school. I've had exposure to new, impressive and creative ideas, with excellent training opportunities and an enthusiasm and energy from staff to innovate for all the right reasons. I've had the opportunity to lead and be led on a range of innovative teaching and learning practices, and a considerable amount of this second edition is born out of those opportunities.

This book is designed to provide practical ideas for getting creative learning and teaching techniques right in both the classroom environment and in the whole-school environment.

This book should provide you with a useful bank of ideas that could be implemented in your classroom and in your wider school to promote a more creative approach to learning. Please do not expect a range of 'off-the-shelf' activities for you simply to emulate in your lessons. There are activities to get you started, but the point of this book is to help you get into a frame of mind that enables you to be more creative under your own steam.

Maybe you are reading this book solely for your own benefit, or maybe you have got together with a team of like-minded teachers to implement strategies and ideas; this book should be helpful in both cases.

1.2 Feeling Creative

You are creative. No excuses, it's official. Creativity is something we all have; we now know that it is a skill that can be learned. It is not simply a gift given to the Mozarts and Einsteins of the world. You might not be as in touch with it as you once were as a child. You might never have had the creative touch nurtured in you in the way that others seem to have had. Or maybe you know there's a creative genius in you that is itching to be let free in the classroom. But take a moment to consider just how creative you and all those people around you actually are.

Think about it – surely a single parent is creative? Managing to cope when one person is doing what two people would normally do. What about your pupils when they go skateboarding or when they're getting excited about things that have happened to them? Surely they've connected with their right brains? What about when you need to work out the solution to a problem? Do you just sit and stress or do you think around the problem to find your solution? What about when you teach? It takes a certain amount of creativity to stand up in front of a class, hold pupils' attention and deliver a lesson. No matter how much more creativity you want to inject into your lessons, you should give yourself some credit here and appreciate what a good job you already do. How many people have told you that they couldn't do what you do? They have the greatest respect for your profession/relentless optimism/bravery and it is down to a certain amount of creativity and perseverance that you have already realized and they have yet to.

Tapping into natural creativity and harnessing it is an excellent way to solve the problems of our twenty-first-century lives. Now more so than ever, because our world today is full of uncertainties – just think of terrorism, increasing awareness about child behavioural issues and the possibilities of technology – all of it makes life in the world at once more exciting and scary.

This is a fundamental reason behind the modern ethic that suggests that pupils today must learn how to learn. If they do so, the theory suggests that pupils in their adult lives will be better placed to handle the twenty-first century's advances and regressions with a creative independence. It is clear that people today no longer learn a trade at school or university and gain a job for life in that field. Everything is constantly evolving, and individuals need to evolve at the same time in order to keep up. Creativity is the key to successful independent learning, and it is through creative teaching that pupils will best get a feel for creative learning. Creative teaching can have many benefits, but it's not just a case of making pupils' learning experience more fun, about 'edutainment'. You can do a great deal to make your pupils' future much brighter by empowering them to know how they learn, and how to learn independently.

Of course, it is not always easy to feel like being creative in the classroom. You might feel tired instead; you've just gone through a pile of marking, your reports are due, and you've got lunch duty to do which eats into your lunch break (which you were going to spend marking and writing reports). It's all very well reading this book, and have me tell you all about how to get creative teaching right, but what's the reality of actually finding the energy to do any of this?

Well, before you put the book down and give up, read this next chapter. It's about how to 'feel' creative. It is necessary to get the conditions right to teach creatively and there are several factors to consider: your pupils, your classroom, even your school, but most importantly there's you. I said earlier that creative teaching does not have to involve spending lots of time preparing things like playing cards or PowerPoint presentations; it is more about how you approach teaching a topic. There's a frame of mind that you can enter into that will, regardless of how tired or stressed you are, overcome any such distractions and enable you to do some fabulous teaching, often quite spontaneously.

I call it your *creative state*.

You can call it what you like, it can't hear you. If you want to call it something more floaty and, well, creative, then you could refer to it as bathing in your *radiant inner glow*. If you want something more down-to-earth, then how about *being-creative-as-opposed-to-being-annoyed-with-your-pupils*? Suffice it to say, I'm going to stick with *creative state*. It's simply a mindset to enter consciously into whenever you walk into a classroom, or approach a scheme of work, a new lesson or even marking.

Let's spend a little time forming this creative state in you. We need to consider a couple of things. First, we need to consider your stress levels and some relaxation techniques. Second, we need to consider how much you know about how people learn, and how this affects your pupils and your teaching. The idea is that whenever you approach your classroom, you will be more conscious of this bank of knowledge and its application and you will combine it with a more relaxed, alert presence of mind. Thus you have the building-blocks of a more successful creative approach.

Later in this book we'll consider more things you may need to be aware of professionally in terms of how you relate to and motivate pupils, the types of activities you set and how you structure your lessons. But before we get into the realms of the practical, let's consider your mindset, your creative state.

1.3 The Causes of Stress

Take any school, from a top private school through to the toughest inner-city school, and there is one thing teachers will have in common: they're stressed to one degree or another. It can be for a whole variety of reasons and at a whole range of levels. In private schools teachers are under enormous pressure to 'magic' top grades out of all their pupils somehow, and any failure to do so is a poor reflection on themselves as professionals. In the toughest inner-city schools, stress often comes from dealing with seriously bad behaviour, whether it is aggression directed towards you, your colleagues or between pupils. In any case there's the report writing and endless marking, the clubs and other extracurricular things you do, dealing with exam boards, stacks of paperwork that never seems to be that constructive, being aware of individual pupils' special needs, chasing homework and coursework, dealing with parents, dealing with senior management (!) and just managing to teach something despite everything else that regularly gets in the way.

Do not think otherwise: teaching is one of the most stressful professions in the world. All that energy from hundreds of pupils: channelled well or badly, it is still energy and young people have it in far more abundance than any adult and, whether it is fun, charming, annoying or terrifying, it can really wear you out. There is all the frustration from dealing with young individuals whose priorities are not your own and which are often quite inconsistent. Most teachers have more right-brain creative leanings than left-brain systematic leanings (why else would you rather work with children than in an office?), so things like staff-room politics and dealing with the administrative side of teaching tend to be a source of aggravation and avoidance rather than something that is par for the course.

So how does stress work? How can it be a good thing and how does it become a bad thing? How do you manage stress as a professional?

Let me tell you a true story.

When I was 18 years old I went on a gap year to Tanzania in East Africa. I worked as a student teacher in a local school in Kilimanjaro. I had a wonderful time and it was this experience that convinced me to go into teaching. Personally, I'm still rather surprised that any of our parents let us all go so far away from home to such a desperately poor area of the world. Anyway, they did and we were better for the experience. However, because we were a group of 18-year-olds in a remote place, there were some stupid occasions. One such occasion was when six of us went on a safari together. We set up our camp for the night, and wandered over to the hippo pool that was there for visitors to watch from a distance.

So there we were, sitting on a bank several hundred yards away from the natural pool, watching three hippos as the sun set. It was charming. We ascertained that we were looking at a little family – mother, father and baby – with the baby hippo sitting on the mother hippo's head. So every few minutes the baby would pop up above the water's surface and then go up another few feet as her mother came up for air too. It was all very amusing and was excellent photo material.

Except Simon and I didn't have good cameras; they lacked any zoom feature.

So, largely because we were 18 and daft, Simon and I decided to venture down the bank for a slightly closer look. In fact, not only did we go to the water's edge, but we also walked along something of a natural jetty. Oh dear.

So Simon and I stood there, at the edge of the natural jetty, with our cameras at the ready, waiting for the shot we were both looking for. And, sure enough, mother and baby hippo popped up in the middle of the lake and we snapped away with our cameras. However, they still felt a little far away in our cameras' viewfinders, so we waited around to see if they would pop up a little closer.

Imagine two 18-year-old boys standing at the water's edge, poised with cameras to their faces, grinning and waiting. Sure enough, mother and baby appeared closer to us. Right in front of us. The mother began to step out of the water, her baby sliding down her back and into the water. She opened her mouth wide and roared at us, vaguely how you might expect a Tyrannosaurus Rex to sound.

We ran.

I ran faster than I had ever run.

I was quite unfit, but somehow I overtook first Simon and then the rest of the group! I travelled hundreds of yards in what felt like seconds, all to avoid certain death in the clutches of a large, smelly hippopotamus. The fear and terror of literally running for my life spurred me on like nothing ever had before or has since. I was superhuman, bounding across the plains of Africa in giant leaps to escape my enemy and claim victory for all humankind. It was a moment of potential glory versus potential gloom. Was I going to succeed? Was I going to survive? I looked behind me to see what carnage the hippo might be creating ...

Fortunately for us, the hippo was just scaring us off, and had not even got out of the water, let alone given chase. If it had decided to run, then there's a strong chance I would not be writing this book, as hippos run faster than humans. Even superhuman versions of me.

Not that I can normally run fast. After about ten yards I begin to feel tired, breathless and rather ashamed of myself. But at that moment I became superhuman, all because there was a mass of adrenalin pumping round my body. I'm sure you are familiar with the term *fight or flight*; well, that's what my story is an example of (and I promise it really is a true story) – my body reacted to the extreme situation with enough adrenalin to pump up my muscles ready either to run away from the hippo or to stay there and stand my ground. Like that would have worked.

The reason for this remarkable natural reaction is all to do with our species' primitive days when this 'fight or flight' response was employed daily against some very physical dangers. While going out to catch dinner, early humans had a lot to contend with and they were constantly fighting for their lives against beasts, the elements and each other. Adrenalin was put to good use, and when it got used it got used up, allowing the body to return to its normal non-superhuman self once the danger has passed.

So when you are faced with a physical stress, adrenalin is released into your bloodstream to give you energy and quick reaction speed. Your blood pressure also rises to force blood into your arms and legs ready to spring into action of some kind. Your heart rate speeds up and circulation to the brain and muscles increases at the expense of the digestive system. The lungs are stimulated for more oxygen and the liver releases sugar. All to get you in a state of readiness to catch dinner, defend your territory, or some other exciting primeval danger.

However, your body will react to any kind of stress in the same way. And most of the time in our modern world the stress we tend to experience is mental stress – that is to say stress caused by what we think. How stressed you get is generally dependent on how different your current situation is from the way you would like it to be.

Mental stress takes lots of forms – it can be about how we are going to fit everything in before all the deadlines hit, about how we are going to deal with that pupil who is always misbehaving, about all the problems we have in our home lives as well as in our professional ones. They all cause adrenalin to start pumping its way around the body ready for you to face the physical challenge of catching dinner. Unfortunately your goal isn't to catch dinner, it's far more cerebral. And in teaching this can be a daily experience.

Tension in the muscles of your body is probably the most obvious response to your mental stress. You may not notice the tension within you, but this does not mean it is not there. Apart from ending up with crease lines on your forehead and face, a tight jaw, clenched fists, tension headaches, backache and a sore neck, tension affects your capacity to function effectively.

One way this can happen is through its effect on your diaphragm. The diaphragm controls your breathing and is particularly vulnerable to tension. A tense diaphragm leads to shallow breathing and consequently to a reduced flow of oxygen to the brain and an increase in certain chemicals in the blood which cause the brain to become sluggish.

Tension can also restrict the flow of blood to the brain, depriving it further of oxygen and nutrients. As a result, your capacity to concentrate, remember, listen and observe is reduced, making you a rather less useful version of yourself than you'd like to be. Which can, of course, cause you more mental stress.

There are fatty acids in your system which don't get burned up because you are not running for your life or catching dinner. Instead they attach themselves to the walls of your arteries and, along with chemicals and other residue, silt up your body cells and inhibit their healthy function. Adrenalin hangs in the system and makes you jumpy, irritable, uptight and on edge. The body goes into a mild form of shock, and the mind becomes foggy and confused.

You can become preoccupied with the sorts of thoughts which cause stress. If you're preoccupied with these thoughts, you will find it very difficult also to focus properly on what you are reading, hearing, studying, marking, planning, teaching and so on. Have you ever put off doing something because you feel that it is too much hassle when you know that is not that difficult to do really?

So basically stress causes physiological problems that affect the way you think, preventing logic from playing any useful part in your mind's activities: your fears and your adrenalin will get the better of you.

Let's do a little test to see how stressed you are. I've listed below a whole load of stressful situations you might be in and given them a stress score out of 100. Tick all the situations that you feel you are in now, or have been in the last six months, or may well be in the next six months. They cover both common personal and professional circumstances. I've provided space for you to add some of your own stressful situations too. Total up the overall stress score; the higher it is, the higher your stress levels. If it comes to over 150, you are stressed – overly stressed. In any case, make sure you read the stress-reducing techniques that follow.

☐ Death of a close family member   100

☐ Death of a close friend   73

☐ Divorce   65

☐ Major personal injury/operation/etc.   63

☐ Getting married   58

☐ Buying a house   55

☐ End of serious long-term relationship   52

☐ Change in health of a family member   48

☐ Sex problems   46

☐ You are pregnant   44

☐ Your partner is pregnant   40

☐ Serious family arguments   39

☐ Second breadwinner loses job   38

☐	Dislike current job	37
☐	New boyfriend or girlfriend	36
☐	Difficulty with behaviour management	35
☐	Increased workload at school	35
☐	Outstanding personal achievement	34
☐	Harassment from a pupil	33
☐	Starting work at a new school	30
☐	Serious argument with senior staff	30
☐	Change in sleeping habits	29
☐	Change in social habits	29
☐	Change in eating habits	28
☐	Minor personal injury	26
☐	Minor traffic violation	20
☐	_____	___
☐	_____	___
☐	_____	___

Stress score   ___

How did you do? You probably scored quite highly. As an anecdotal guide, this list is quite good because it is hard to quantify stress levels and this tool allows you to get some idea of just how much stress you could legitimately be feeling.

Personal management is essentially to be able to use your creative state successfully. Primary to that is being able to manage your stress levels: knowing your boundaries, recognizing when you've gone past those boundaries and being able to handle those situations. It's about being able to react from the head, instead of emotionally. Or, better still, to be able to predict the situation rather than react to it.

Dealing with stress: an awareness strategy

There are a number of ways to deal with stress, starting from a simple awareness strategy, and then on to ways to deal with stress as it happens, and finally more preventative measures you can take.

It's very hard to spot the moment you become stressed about something. It can take different forms: for example, anger towards a misbehaving pupil or a lack of focus caused by lots of deadlines. Two different situations, two different reactions, but one physiological response: stress and tension.

If you find yourself snapping a lot at your pupils, or showing other signs of stress, but you are unaware of the causes or when you start to show signs of stress, then you could try giving yourself a running commentary about your emotional state.

I'm feeling very tired,

pupil x is doing such-and-such,

it annoys me because ...

I want to shout at him and say ...

It's not a terribly natural thing to do, obviously, but try it for a day, or even an hour, to gauge how you react to situations. A running commentary requires you to be logical, so you might find yourself judging your reactions as they occur, or before they occur. This might stop you from doing something you might regret, from overreacting, or it may well justify your actions entirely. But at least you'll be more aware of what was causing your stress.

As for facing workload issues such as marking, report writing and the large pile of paperwork, consider first making sure that you have prioritized everything. Simply write a list of everything that needs to be done and order it in terms of imminence and the time you estimate it will require. You could start by grading things A, B and C in terms of their importance, and then numbering them off in the order that you will approach them. This way you will have a much clearer idea as to why and when you should tackle certain bits of paperwork.

As for report-writing, do not feel guilty about preparing several basic reports and then adapting the relevant report to a pupil. It gives you a valid framework to start from and can do a lot to remove the pressure of writing reports.

Dealing with stress as it happens

There are all sorts of possible scenarios here. You could be at home thinking about problems at work; you could be at school facing a pupil who is about to get the better of you; you could be feeling that you just can't be bothered; you could be feeling angry or upset; or it could all just be getting a bit too much for you. Whatever situation you find yourself in, here are a few simple ideas to deal with all that adrenalin and stress and be a bit better prepared to enter into your creative state.

Breathe properly. Stress will cause a tense diaphragm, which will in turn make your breathing shallow and your brain more sluggish. By taking control of your breathing you can relax the diaphragm muscles and stop stress from getting a tighter hold. Essentially you are preventing your more primitive, dinner-hunting instincts from taking over by being properly self-aware.

Simply breathe in to the count of three, hold it for the count of three, and let it out slowly to the count of five. People vary in whether they prefer to do this through the mouth or nose. You should do as you please. The point here is to get rid of shallow breathing, filling up your lungs and relaxing tense muscles. You can also use this when you are having trouble getting to sleep. Instead of churning round lots of stressful thoughts in your mind, focus instead on breathing properly.

Another idea is to count to six every time you feel that you are about to snap at someone. In that time, your left brain will have had a chance to kick in and assess whether it is really worth your while getting stressed about the situation or whether there is a more peaceful solution. Given that stress is caused by your perception of the situation you are in or are thinking about, then it stands to reason that you can remove stress by assessing the situation more logically, accurately or positively. On what I would hope is an obvious note, this does not negate situations when a genuine stress response is needed: if a pack of wild dogs (or pupils) is chasing after you, then please don't try counting or looking at the positive side, just run and run fast!

Notice that there are two basic principles used here so far: the first strategy (breathing) deals with the physiological aspect of stress – that is to say, it deals with the effect it has on your body by doing an activity to dissipate it. The second strategy (counting to six) is basically mind over matter – it deals with the psychological aspect of stress and uses reason to tell the mind that it does not need to feel stressed. Be ready to apply these general principles when trying to deal with stress.

A more thorough method to deal with the physiological aspect of stress is to exercise. While mental stress does not elicit the need to fight or flee, your body is tensed up ready to do something physical. So do something physical if you can. Many schools allow teachers to use their sports facilities, so pull some weights or go swimming; alternatively go for a jog or a brisk walk. Or you could do some exercises in your home such as press-ups, crunches, jogging on the spot, or even yoga. Yoga? Yes, yoga. Here are two exercises for you to try, or to try with your classes:

The eagle stretch

Stage 1 pose

- Stand with your feet together.

- Check your arms: which one is right and which is left, don't mix them up!

- Bring your right arm under your left arm, crossing at the elbow.

- Twist your right hand towards your face and around the left forearm.

- Place your right palm against the left palm, perfectly flat to each other, fingertips to fingertips.

- Keep your palms flat against each other and your chin up. Lower your shoulders and pull down your arms, bringing them towards your chest.

- Fit your mini-steeple nicely under your nose like an eagle's beak! This might be rather tricky at first, but you will get better at it I'm sure.

Stage 2 pose

Keep your feet together, spine straight, and your heels on the floor. Bend your knees about six inches until you feel a healthy pull. Look at a point in front of you and focus on it so that you don't fall over.

Now transfer your weight to your left leg and slowly lift your right leg up high. Bring your right leg over your left thigh and wrap your right leg's calf and foot around the lower part of your left leg. The top of your big toe should hook around the left leg's ankle.

Why?

The eagle stretch improves blood flow to the kidneys, helps firm calves, thighs, hips and abdominal muscles. It also increases blood flow to your brain, which improves concentration and alertness.

The awkward stretch

Stage 1 pose

- Stand with your feet about six inches apart, heels and toes nice and straight.

- Raise your arms in front of you, parallel with the floor, palms down, fingers together, arms and hands about six inches apart.

- Look at one point in front of you that is at eye level and keep focused on that point.

- Keep your heels flat on the floor and knees apart, sit down until the backs of your thighs are parallel with the floor and stop there. (Pretend there is a chair behind you and you are sitting on it.)

Stage 2 pose

Now arch your spine back, aiming for a perfectly straight spine, as though your back were against a wall. To do this, put your weight on your heels, raising your toes off the floor as you arch your back. Keep toes, heels, knees and hands all six inches apart, hold this pose to the count of ten.

Stage 3 pose

Slowly come up. Still keeping hands, arms and feet all six inches apart, and arms parallel to floor, stand up on your toes.

Why?

The awkward stretch increases blood circulation in knees and ankle joints. It strengthens and firms all muscles of the thighs, calves, hips and arms. And it gets your blood pumping, increasing the flow of blood to your brain.

It's all in the mind

So that's some physical strategies. What about some psychological ones? Well, by far and away the most popular one is visual imagery. Modern-day mental stress is caused by what you think, so think of something else. Select a scenario in your mind that makes you smile and relax, and then think of it whenever things are getting a bit too much. It might be a nice beach or other holiday spot where you felt relaxed. Or it could be a funny moment from a film, book or real life that just makes you smile. These ideas are designed to help you regain perspective, to stop you making a challenge become a threat or even a catastrophe. At the end of a bad lesson, when you can feel the stress getting to you, just ask yourself, 'Did the world end?' If it didn't, and nobody got injured, then congratulate yourself – it could have been much worse.

Long-term strategies

The best strategies for dealing with stress work when you combine the physical and psychological strategies. Any activity that combines mind and body will help you tremendously. Going out for the night with friends should be a great stress relief – you get the chance to enjoy talking with friends and the physical exercise of dancing, walking, paintballing or whatever else you like to get up to at the weekend. I'm sure you'll be glad to have it confirmed that sex is an excellent form of stress relief, particularly when it is with someone special to you because of the psychological connection you have. Failing that, then meditation will work well, particularly in the form of something like T'ai Chi, which combines your thoughts and your actions into a peaceful state.

However you choose to relax, it is important to think of life as a process to go through. You tend to think that deadlines, pupils, paperwork, management and so on cause you mental stress, but they don't. Your thoughts cause you stress: what you think about these things; how you evaluate them in your mind.

A common evaluation is to see consequences as 'horrible'. 'Horriblizing' the consequences of your behaviour is what causes most mental stress. The less stressful alternative is to think of these consequences as being 'unfortunate' (rather than horrible), and maybe even 'predictable'. The bottom line is that if you put whatever dedication and work is required into achieving a more creative classroom, then you'll probably get it. If you don't put in the work, or don't acquire the necessary skills and strategies, then there's not a lot of sense in worrying about the predictable outcome.

1.4 Fixed and Growth Mindset

Carol Dweck's now famous work on mindsets (2006) reveals something fundamental about the way in which we approach problems. She identifies two broad mindsets that people get themselves into. People with a fixed mindset tend to believe that the way things are currently is the way they will remain. They believe that you are naturally predisposed to be a talented athlete, musician, entrepreneur, artist, charity worker, politician, teacher, and so on. They fail to notice the '10,000 hours' of practice Michael Jordan puts in to being an excellent basketball player, or the years of toiling away that Sir Alan Sugar put in to growing his business from scratch. People such as Jordan and Sugar have growth mindsets: the idea that – within reason – you can achieve what you want to if you are willing to work hard at it.

If you or your pupils see the world through a fixed mindset, then you are automatically setting yourself up for stress. The world requires you to have a growth mindset – to continue to push yourself, to learn and to adapt to new challenges and skills. Fixed-mindset people live in a world where personality, intelligence, leadership and sporting ability all are fixed. Fixed-mindset people see these things as outside their control. They believe that people are either sociable or not, well behaved or not, gifted or not, talented or not, and so on. And something called the confirmation bias, a tendency we all have to see evidence for the things we believe and not to notice the evidence that would disprove those beliefs, reaffirms those fixed ideas.

The problem is that people with a fixed mindset avoid putting the effort into things they think they're no good at. And to add to the problem they tend to avoid taking risks so as to avoid failure in something they are meant to be naturally good at – so they don't push themselves here either.

Someone with a growth mindset believes that personality develops, intelligence grows, and leadership and sporting ability improves with experience. This means that all these things are within your control. Making mistakes becomes an important part of the learning process, not a sign of weakness. Someone with a growth mindset is still realistic – if you weigh 30 stone you are not going to run a marathon next week. But having a growth mindset enables you to realize that change is unlikely if you don't try. Go to YouTube and search for 'Team Hoyt' to see a father and son overcome extraordinary adversity simply because they both had a growth mindset. I have provided a link to this video on the companion website.

In the classroom, this means that you should praise effort, not ability. The term 'gifted and talented' is a terrible one as it suggests that those your school has put into that group do not need to continue to put in the effort. It encourages a fixed mindset. Don't praise pupils for being 'naturally gifted' in your subject – can you really be sure that producing the outstanding work they do is effortless? Instead say that such pupils 'thrive on the challenges' of your subject and that they put in an 'outstanding effort' that really pays off.

But what about you? What's your mindset? It won't come as much of a surprise that a successfully creative teacher will need a growth mindset themselves; and will need to encourage growth mindsets in their pupils. You can take Carol Dweck's Mindset Test online at mindsetonline.com/testyourmindset/index.html.

1.5 Entering your Creative State

So in order to be successfully creative you need to be willing to enter a growth mindset and you need to be calm. Not so calm that you have become docile – you need to remain alert and on the ball – just calm enough to accept that your pupils might be noisier, might be out of their seats, might have to work together, might not do any writing, or whatever other things you have normally expected to do in a lesson. You need to be prepared to manage such situations calmly, and with good, positive behaviour-management strategies in place. As soon as you show agitation, you suggest to pupils that you are not in control of yourself or the class, and this can become an opportunity for less motivated pupils to sabotage your efforts.

Self-talk is a good place to start. As you walk to your classroom, tell yourself something to get yourself motivated. I suggest it's something that makes you smile. Tell yourself that you're fab, that you are a creative genius, a mastermind of your subject (which is, of course, the best subject in the world) and the epitome of calm, emotional stability in a world of never ending possibilities. Got the idea?!

It also helps if you visualize your class, how you are going to address them and what activities you are going to do with them.

Tell yourself (and them) that you think they are all marvellous (even if they are not), and think of calm, non-confrontational ways you can anticipate and prevent bad behaviour. More advice on dealing with behaviour can be found in Sue Cowley's excellent *Getting the Buggers to Behave* (2011).

Of course, this mental preparation is only any use if you have something to put into practice with your pupils. There are certain fundamental educational theories about creativity and pupils that you need to know about and employ in your teaching. In themselves they should help you feel creative. Below I will outline more about how the brain learns and I will explain some major theories. Later in the book I will give you practical advice about applying these theories in your classroom and in your school. By theories, I refer to the more scientific use of the word: a valid concept that has been tested and in support of which there is considerable proof, that is still open to further investigation, but that is no longer seriously open to being disproved or disregarded. Like the big bang theory, for instance.

1.6 Creativity and Learning

Learning is not something that happens to pupils. They are not passive vessels to be filled up with information. They are not sponges that soak up every word you utter. They might have been when younger, but at secondary school they become selective. Their RAS has kicked in and will discard information or activity that does not get their attention – the same as you would. As they grow up they want to be treated more like adults, and that means they also need to take responsibility for their actions.

As teachers we are quick to apply this rule to their behaviour, but what about their learning behaviour? Surely if we expect them to act responsibly in the classroom, then we should expect them to learn with a sense of responsibility too? Nurturing a sense of ownership of and self-development through their work is a crucial part of creative learning. Unless they do so, pupils will continue to be passive creatures and will never develop the level of autonomy and improved learning performance of which they are capable.

Knowing how to learn can unlock all sorts of possibilities in pupils. If they learn the study skills of how the brain processes information, how they can participate more actively in the learning process, what their preferred learning styles are, and how to revise effectively, then they can be empowered to take more interest in and responsibility for their work and there can be real improvement in their learning performance.

We've already touched on the reticular activating system (RAS) and the right (creative) and left (logical) parts of the brain. But how does the brain actually learn?

Neural pathways

A neuron is a brain cell that we can use to store and process information (that is to say, we think using cells called neurons). One neuron connects with other neurons and forms a tiny electrical current between those cells, a neural pathway. It is fair (if not completely accurate) to say that this neural pathway represents a piece of information, a

The more things you learn, the more neural pathways you form in your mind. These pathways link up with other related pathways and as a result you will develop a better understanding of the material you are learning about, and you'll be able to form opinions and insights about it.

In order to memorize that information, you need to reinforce it by reviewing it now and again. Doing this makes that neural pathway light up in your brain and become stronger. The more times you light up those neural pathways, the quicker your brain will find the information and the longer it will stay accessible to your memory.

At this point I could start talking in more detailed technical terms, mentioning axons, dendrites and synapses. But I'm sure that you don't have all day to read about this. Suffice it to say that an axon is a neuron's transmitter and dendrites are a neuron's receptors. The synaptic cleft is the tiny gap formed between connecting axons and dendrites that allows the electrical signal (otherwise known as a thought) to go from the transmitting neuron to the receiving neuron. A single neuron can receive signals from thousands of other neurons all at once. That neuron may then transmit an electrical signal to thousands of other neurons and the process of thinking takes place.

Our brains are, by and large, the same. They all have about the same number of brain cells as each other, so good news: you have something in common with Einstein after all. And so do all your pupils. You see, it's not the number of brain cells that

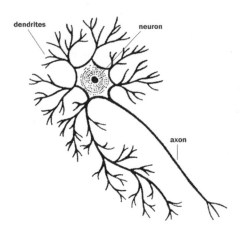

is important, it's the number of connections you make between them that counts. You may well have more neurons than there are stars in the Milky Way (you really do), but if you're not using them effectively, you won't be so bright!

Einstein made more than the average number of neural connections in order to be as clever as he was, and we all have the potential to do the same. Obviously, the connections you make are often affected by your experiences, particularly in childhood, and the more pathways that are formed and strengthened early on in life, the better. Likewise, what you eat, how much you sleep, and the perceptions you hold are all contributory factors to the effectiveness of your neural network.

It is fair to say that the make-up of each individual's brain is unique. Your brain consists of a range of faculties that are reasonably separate from each other – they certainly occupy different areas of the brain – and that have developed depending on the stimuli they have received. Such faculties include things like speaking, comprehending, reading, writing, spatial orientation, singing, and being able to relate to people. In people who have suffered damage to certain parts of the brain only certain faculties are disrupted and others continue to function normally. Your brain is not really one entity; it is a series of abilities that form connections to work together according to your experiences, your genes and your environment.

These connections and these abilities are not static: they can always be made better or worse, and as such there is a gap to be bridged between a student's current learning performance and his or her potential learning performance. Our goal as teachers is to stimulate and activate those neurons and those abilities. Of course you can't force a student to make and then strengthen neural connections, but you can motivate students to do so themselves.

VAK

We all learn by seeing, hearing and doing. In more formal language, we all learn through our visual, auditory and kinaesthetic channels. These channels can work together. However, most people are likely to prefer one channel to the other two; this is referred to as your preferred learning channel or style. There are reasonably straightforward tests available to help students determine their preferred learning channel.

Research shows that there is a fairly even three-way split between people's channel preferences. A study of 5,300 students by Specific Diagnostic Studies Inc. of Rockville, Maryland, (1999) revealed that in any class in any subject in any school there tends to be on average:

- 29% students with a visual preference

- 34% students with a auditory preference

- 37% students with a kinaesthetic preference

Essentially, the evidence from the last 30 years of research in this area (Bandler and Grinder developed this concept as part of their Neuro-Linguistic Programming project in the 1970s) suggests that those students of yours who insist on rocking on the back legs of their chairs and flicking bits of paper across the room would actually take part in your lessons and learn if they were able to participate in an active, kinaesthetic way (Bandler and Grinder, 1981).

Don't panic, we're not about to suggest that all teachers have to start competing with the Art or PE departments for the messiest/ most active classroom in the school; there are plenty of simple and easy ways to incorporate kinaesthesia in teaching and learning. The impact of feeling excluded from learning, by not being 'clever' enough to understand academic (visual–auditory) teaching and learning, cannot be underestimated.

You probably have plenty of visual and auditory activities in your lessons. Visual activities like reading, drawing and writing are extremely valuable learning tools. Auditory activities like giving a talk, listening to you and each other, are again extremely useful skills. You also get television documentaries and PowerPoint presentations which combine visual and auditory channels – again, great. I'm not suggesting for one minute that any of these activities should be discarded – after all, we all learn through all three learning channels.

However, there is much to be said for incorporating the kinaesthetic. Some activities are wholly kinaesthetic – like doing actions to keywords or ideas to remember, or creating role-plays or a tableau of an event. Others neatly combine with the other two styles: a discussion where pupils have to move around the room from one person to another; or a creative writing exercise where the pupil has to imagine him- or herself in a given situation. The best kinaesthetic activities involve the pupil as directly as possible in the content to be learned – it gives them a relevant context, a hook, a handle, to comprehend and learn.

FACT BOX – PREFERRED LEARNING STYLES AND TEACHING

Your own preferred learning style will affect your teaching style. Teachers with an auditory preference tend to do a lot more talking to (or rather, at) the class than do more visual or kinaesthetic teachers. Teachers with a kinaesthetic preference are easy to spot: they are the teachers who sit on their desks and don't mind a bit of noise from their class. Teachers with a visual preference are far more likely than their colleagues to have lots of bright, colourful displays on their walls. You may of course be well-balanced between all three styles.

Of course, learning preferences are not fixed, nor are they an exact science. You can take a quiz to see where your preferences might lie, and this will give you a good indication, but you will know best yourself when you reflect on how you conduct yourself in the classroom – what do you prefer doing? It's important to note that pupils cannot use their preferred learning style as an excuse for not working or doing certain tasks in your lessons. If you think about it, we all learn by seeing, hearing and doing. The point here is to get you to consider which of these three styles you might be neglecting in your teaching, and if you would like your pupils to do the quiz too then they can consider how best to go about their revision and their own learning outside the classroom.

Here's a preferred learning styles quiz to take. Tick or highlight your most likely reaction to each situation. Try to avoid ticking more than one – you are looking to assess your first response to a situation, not all of your responses! Then count up the number of Vs, As and Ks your scored. The one with the highest score is your preferred learning style, followed by your second and then your least liked style.

What do you notice most about people?
- ☐ V how they look or dress?
- ☐ A how they sound when they talk?
- ☐ K how they stand or move?

How do you learn most easily?
- ☐ V by reading and observing?
- ☐ A by being told what to do?
- ☐ K by getting stuck in and doing it for yourself?

If you had to wait for a bus, would you probably:
- [ ] V watch and admire the scenery, or read?
- [ ] A talk to or phone people?
- [ ] K walk around and fidget?

What would make you think someone was lying?
- [ ] V the way they look, or avoid looking, at you?
- [ ] A their tone of voice?
- [ ] K a feeling you get about their sincerity?

When you have many things to do, do you:
- [ ] V make lists for yourself?
- [ ] A keep reminding yourself you have things to do?
- [ ] K feel restless until all or most of the things are done?

What kind of humour do you prefer?
- [ ] V cartoons/comics?
- [ ] A stand-up comedians?
- [ ] K slapstick?

At a party do you tend to spend most of your time:
- [ ] V watching what is happening?
- [ ] A talking and listening to others?
- [ ] K circulating around or dancing?

When you are learning, do you prefer:
- [ ] V work that is written and drawn in colour?
- [ ] A to listen to a talk or be told what to do?
- [ ] K to be active: making and doing?

You solve problems most easily by:
- [ ] V writing or drawing out possible solutions
- [ ] A talking through possible solutions
- [ ] K getting stuck in and working it out as you go

When you are angry, do you:
- ☐ V silently seethe inside?
- ☐ A shout and scream?
- ☐ K clench your fists, grit your teeth, stomp about and go away angry?

Your preferred/favourite way to relax is:
- ☐ V watch TV or read
- ☐ A listen to the radio/music
- ☐ K do a physical activity (e.g. playing sport)

When trying to remember people, do you tend to:
- ☐ V remember faces, but forget names?
- ☐ A remember names, but forget faces?
- ☐ K remember things I did with them?

In a video shop you are more likely to rent:
- ☐ V action adventure
- ☐ A musicals
- ☐ K dramas

You try to spell a new or difficult word by:
- ☐ V writing it to see how it looks
- ☐ A sounding it out
- ☐ K writing it to see how it feels

Total number of Vs _____
Total number of As _____
Total number of Ks _____

Multiple intelligences

Earlier I mentioned that the brain is a series of fairly separate faculties that work together. Howard Gardner famously developed his theory of Multiple Intelligences in line with this thinking. Essentially Gardner (1999) defines intelligence as an ability or potential to solve problems or create something in a way that is beneficial (in whatever context one is in – from the classroom to the whole world).

Having noticed that people seem to be clever in different ways – just compare Mozart to Newton – he went about assessing ways in which people could be intelligent. He used a set of eight testable criteria, which included things like psychological tasks and questions such as *does it have a dedicated area of the brain?* He originally concluded that there were seven intelligences, and has since appended an eighth.

First you have your academic intelligences: *linguistic intelligence*, which involves spoken and written language and its use and is the province of lawyers, speakers, writers, poets, translators and the like; and *logical–mathematical intelligence*, which involves the ability to analyse problems logically and is the domain of mathematicians, logicians and scientists.

Next there are the more artistic intelligences. *Musical intelligence* deals with areas such as performance, composition and appreciation of musical patterns. Gardner noted that the patterns of understanding music are very similar to that of language, and he therefore saw no reason why he should regard the latter as an intelligence and the former as a talent. *Bodily kinaesthetic intelligence* refers to those who use their bodies to solve problems or create things, such as dancers, actors, athletes, craftsmen, surgeons and mechanics. *Spatial intelligence* is about the ability to recognize and manipulate patterns of space, whether they be small (think sculptors and surgeons) or big (think aeroplane pilots).

Then there are the personal intelligences: *interpersonal* and *intrapersonal*. Interpersonal intelligence is the ability to understand people's intentions, motivations and desires and/or to be able to work with them. Salespeople, teachers, actors, religious leaders and political leaders are all good examples of people who possess interpersonal intelligence. *Intrapersonal intelligence* refers to your ability to know and understand yourself, your desires, fears and capacities and is measured not by people's jobs and activities, but by how well you can regulate your own life.

Gardner endorsed an eighth intelligence (and is happy for there to be more, provided that they meet his criteria). This eighth intelligence is the *naturalist intelligence*, demonstrated by how well one understands the patterns of the physical world, recognizes species and spots relations, and/or is able to care for, tame or interact with living creatures. Hunters, fishermen, farmers, gardeners, cooks, biologists and of course naturalists all exhibit naturalist intelligence.

Gardner has also been tempted to add a ninth intelligence, the *existential intelligence*, which would deal with one's ability to appreciate and tackle the big questions of existence, but there is not quite enough proof that this ability merits separate treatment from the other eight intelligences. A good existential philosopher would draw on their naturalist, linguistic, interpersonal and intrapersonal intelligences.

Bear in mind that each intelligence will have different end results in different people: I may have musical intelligence, but that doesn't make me Mozart. Wayne Sleep may have bodily kinaesthetic intelligence, but that doesn't mean he would be any good as a surgeon. Each intelligence is something of an umbrella term for a range of subintelligences which, when nurtured and combined with other subintelligences, will form a unique neural circuitry that will make that person good at whatever they are good at.

The point of knowing about this in the context of creative teaching is that you can, of course, tap into pupils' intelligences to engage with them better and to help them learn. Using narratives is good for linguistic intelligence; using deductive reasoning helps with logical–mathematical intelligence, as does denoting the connections between items of information your pupils are learning; using art, music and other things aesthetic helps with the arts-based intelligences; doing something hands-on, such as visiting a museum or performing experiments, is good for bodily kinaesthetic intelligence and doing something social like group-based discovery tasks is good for both personal intelligences.

However, you should be slightly wary about testing pupils to find their multiple intelligences and then labelling them accordingly. By all means test your pupils to find out which intelligences they have strengths in, but do so in an intelligence-specific way. Most MI tests available are tickbox pencil-and-pen tests, which by their nature are linguistic and logical–mathematical, and are therefore not accurate measuring tools for all the other intelligences. To measure someone's musical intelligence, see how well they can recognize or sing a tune; to measure someone's spatial intelligence, see how they perform on a Duke of Edinburgh Scheme field trip.

It is also unwise to try to quantify how intelligent someone is in each area – for example, to say that you are 35 per cent interpersonally intelligent, 25 per cent linguistically intelligent and so on. Multiple intelligences are not static, particularly among your pupils, and they will change as pupils make progress. It should be sufficient to identify ability in areas and give support in the development of that intelligence, as well as improve weaker areas too.

Neither is it necessary to teach the same thing in eight different ways to suit each intelligence. It is both unnecessary and impractical. But the more angles you can give to learning a topic, then the more likely pupils will understand and memorize it. So the creative teacher needs to think of what intelligences can be drawn upon appropriately to help pupils learn a given topic. And once you've taught it, you need to evaluate how it went and what could be improved next time around. It is not as though failing to teach something via a particular learning style equates with a pupil's failure to learn. Everyone learns in a multitude of ways, and multiple intelligences provide a good checklist to use to ensure that you are using a range of engaging methods.

More ideally, learning is personalized to each of your pupils. Imagine if your school had completed an appropriate MI test, and a VAK test, and you knew your pupils' learning strengths and weaknesses. You could then set different forms of learning activities for pupils to play to their strengths or improve weaker areas as appropriate. Marvellous. But the reality is that this is too big an ask of teachers, it requires time and resources beyond our current education system. And to be applied properly, the national curriculum would have to, at least, become a lot more flexible to allow pupils to excel in subjects more appropriate to their intellectual abilities. Not likely. But when opportunities arise to get to know your pupils' personalities, then take it and ask them about what they enjoy doing. It might give you some insight into their intelligences and what learning methods might be appropriate to them, and give you some ideas for activities to do with your class or with that pupil when they seem to be struggling. I've included ideas and templates in the Creative Classroom section to help you get started.

VAK and Multiple Intelligences are complementary, not conflicting, theories. Think of VAK as a different perspective on what happens in your classroom. You might prefer to think in terms of VAK when planning a lesson or a scheme of work, or you might prefer to think in terms of MI, or both. As long as there is variety in approach, then pupils will be better engaged and have more opportunities to get to grips with your subject. Both of these theories provide you with resources and frameworks to create that variety; it all comes down to personal preference.

1.7 Emotional Intelligence, Character Strengths, Wellbeing and Learning

The next area I would like to look at in this section is the role of emotions and personality in the classroom. It might be an obvious statement to make, but your pupils are not all the same. There are differences in personality, differences in age, differences in maturity and differences in emotional wellbeing – that is to say the degree to which someone feels happy, safe and secure in themselves and in their environment. Not only that, but you yourself need to consider how your personality, age, maturity and emotional wellbeing impact upon your pupils. There are different, complementary, ways to consider these areas and I'd like to focus particularly on Emotional Intelligence, as developed by Mayer and Salovey and popularized by Goleman (1996), and Character Strengths, as developed by positive psychologist Martin Seligman (2011) and his team at the University of Pennsylvania (2007).

Emotional Intelligence

Emotional Intelligence is not linked directly with Multiple Intelligences, but it does focus upon interpersonal and intrapersonal intelligences. It is appropriate here because it encapsulates something about your psyche and that of the pupils and colleagues you know. Developed by two psychologists from the USA, Mayer and Salovey (2004), it has become something of a well-established concept in both business and education. Emotional Intelligence, or EI or EQ, is to do with your ability to perceive, understand and express your feelings accurately and to control your emotions so that they work for you and not against you. It is all about self-awareness and empathy.

This is important in creative teaching on two counts: for your own EI and to develop your pupils' EI. Schools that aim to develop their pupils' emotional and social awareness will focus on, among other things, enabling pupils to recognize their emotional states, developing empathy by identifying non-verbal clues as to how someone feels, managing stress, understanding what motivates and demotivates them, improving listening skills and learning and applying conflict resolution strategies. The University of Illinois at Chicago tested schools committed to teaching such strategies and demonstrated that 50 per cent of pupils improved academically, misbehaviour dropped by an average of 28 per cent, and exclusions by 44 per cent. 63 per cent of pupils demonstrated considerably more positive behaviour. All of this was attributed to the success of their EI projects.

EI should not be mistaken for a revolutionary new concept. It enshrines something in scientific terms that resonates with religious beliefs, philosophy and society throughout time. Aristotle once said that anyone can become angry – that is easy. But to be angry with the right person, to the right degree, at the right time, for the right purpose, and in the right way – that is not easy. Aristotle's point here is that our feelings often get in the way; they seem to hijack thoughts and reactions from the more intellectual areas of our brain and replace them with thoughts and reactions from our lower brain functions instead. When you should react with sympathy and solutions, you go into 'fight or flight' mode.

As a creative teacher it is important that you have a high EQ (as opposed to IQ) so that you can manage yourself effectively. We've already looked a how stress affects you, so what about the rest of your emotions? Being self-aware and in control of yourself will ensure that you can create a safe, creative and empowering environment for your pupils. There are numerous EQ tests online that you could use, such as the Mayer-Salovey-Caruso Emotional Intelligence Test (MSCEIT), but I would encourage you simply to reflect on how aware you are of your emotional state and what you do to manage it. Salovey and Mayer proposed a model that used four branches of emotional intelligence, each one going a stage deeper into your ability to handle emotions:

- your perception of emotions: you are able to detect emotions in people's faces and voices, etc;

- your use of emotions: you are able to use your mood to best facilitate the things you do, such as problem-solving, thinking and being creative;

- your understanding of emotions: one step beyond perception, you are able to pick up on the emotional messages people send out and change what you do or say in response to bring about the best possible outcome, you understand how one emotion can lead to another such as anger to shame or like to love, and you understand how one emotion can trigger certain behaviour in yourself and in others;

- your management of emotions: you are able to judge whether an emotion is going to be useful or a hindrance in a situation and enhance positive emotions without repressing negative ones, and you can help others to identify their emotions and benefit from them.

So when you feel yourself getting angry at a misbehaving pupil you have to ask yourself 'will anger be the most beneficial response?' It might be. Maybe a short sharp shock from you would be all that's needed. But I tend to find that pupils who often misbehave will feed off your anger and so would enjoy upsetting you further, in which case anger won't be the most useful response. Also, if you often feel angry in these situations, then it isn't good for your own wellbeing and job satisfaction, and so there might be other ways of dealing with it.

There are many books out there about behaviour management, and the best of them essentially require an emotionally intelligent approach. Being fair, clear, approachable and consistent makes a crucial difference to how creative you can be in the classroom. But by fair I don't mean a one-size-fits-all policy. In my pastoral experience, I have seen both teacher and pupil display a remarkable lack of self-awareness and/or empathy. The teacher who, despite knowing that a pupil's parent is terminally ill, gives a detention for not handing in a piece of work on time. The pupil who has anger management issues and doesn't realize this is connected to their difficult childhood. Being fair and emotionally intelligent means responding to the *individual*. It means listening, not just hearing, and it means being open to changing your mind. Remember: sympathy and solutions.

FACT BOX – CONSIDER YOUR EMOTIONAL INTELLIGENCE

Rank each of the areas of emotional intelligence identified above according to how well you feel you do them now by circling the appropriate number. Try to think of examples where you have found yourself in these situations.

Area of Emotional Intelligence:	Area to develop		I do this well	
Your perception of emotions: you are able to detect emotions in people's faces and voices	1	2	3	4
Your use of emotions: you are able to use your mood to facilitate the things such as problem-solving, thinking and being creative	1	2	3	4

	1	2	3	4
Your understanding of emotions: you are able to pick up on the emotional messages people send out and change what you do or say in response to bring about the best possible outcome	1	2	3	4
your understanding of emotions: you understand how one emotion can lead to another such as anger to shame or like to love, and you understand how one emotion can trigger certain behaviour in yourself and in others	1	2	3	4
your management of emotions: you are able to judge whether an emotion is going to be useful or a hindrance in a situation, and to enhance positive emotions without repressing negative ones	1	2	3	4
your management of emotions: you can help others identify their emotions and benefit from them	1	2	3	4

Character Strengths

Martin Seligman and his team of psychologists from the University of Pennsylvania decided that psychology had spent too long considering what was wrong with people, and wanted to identify what was right with people. They researched and identified 24 character strengths, or virtues in action, that are universal – regardless of culture or other social factors. They developed a test that you can do to identify what your top five character strengths are. You can do it for free online at www. viasurvey.org.

They placed the various character strengths into six groups. Here they are:

Strengths of Wisdom and Knowledge:

- creativity [originality, ingenuity]
- curiosity [interest, novelty-seeking, openness to experience]
- open-mindedness [judgement, critical thinking]
- love of learning
- perspective [wisdom]

Strengths of Courage:

- bravery
- persistence [perseverance, industriousness]
- integrity [authenticity, honesty]
- vitality [zest, enthusiasm, vigour, energy]

Strengths of Humanity (interpersonal strengths that involve tending to and befriending others):

- love

- kindness [generosity, nurture, care, compassion, altruism, "niceness"]
- social intelligence [emotional intelligence, personal intelligence]

Strengths of Justice:

- citizenship [social responsibility, loyalty, teamwork]
- fairness
- leadership

Strengths of Temperance: strengths that protect against excess:

- forgiveness and mercy
- humility / modesty
- prudence
- self-regulation [self-control]

Strengths of Transcendence:

- appreciation of beauty and excellence [awe, wonder, elevation]
- gratitude
- hope [optimism, future-mindedness, future orientation]
- humour [playfulness]
- spirituality [religiousness, faith, coherency of belief and purpose]

Think of all the pupils you teach. Which ones are the most modest? Which ones are the most grateful? Humorous? Kind? Open-minded? Creative? Fair? Which ones display the flip side of some of these strengths, or the 'shadow side' as Seligman's team like to call it? This is a fairly radical way of looking at our pupils. Traditionally pupils were sponges whose job was to soak up information and spill it out again when squeezed for it. In more modern times, the whole child is to be taken into consideration. This has come to mean making personalized learning plans and having a special educational needs register. What I'm suggesting here, and I would welcome more research on this, is how much pupils' positive character traits influence their learning and the classroom dynamic. But what you can measure right now are your positive character strengths by going to that website and taking its test. How can you build on your top strengths in your teaching, and how can you develop some of your lower-scoring strengths through more creative teaching?

Wellbeing

Pupils often find it funny that their teachers have a life outside of the classroom – think of the pupil that will tell you that they saw you in Tesco or wherever. But it is also really easy for us teachers to forget that the children in your classroom have a life outside of the classroom. Not only have they just learned a hundred and one other things since your last lesson, but there may well be personal issues at home or with friends that are playing on their minds. Or maybe they'd just rather be watching the telly.

How well pupils cope with being told that they got the wrong answer, or that their work wasn't good enough, or that they must try harder will depend on many of the things we've looked at in this section, and how frequently they hear these things. But you must be aware that the more a pupil feels like a failure, the less resilient they will be and ultimately they will become a self-fulfilling prophecy. Think about any bad patterns of behaviour you and your pupils have got in to. There was a boy I taught whose bad behaviour was very annoying, but I chose to ignore it and focus instead on a good piece of work he produced for me. When he was out of line, I asked him to correct his behaviour, I didn't complain about him. After a while, when he realized I wasn't making any personal judgements about him, his behaviour for me improved. To be honest with you, I was making judgements, but I kept them to myself! It came as quite a revelation to me when he came to me to tell me about a personal issue that explained a lot of his bad behaviour, citing that I was the only teacher he felt wouldn't judge him. The episode made me really appreciate the difference that the things teachers say to their pupils can make.

Please consider your pupils' feelings when giving feedback in any form. Smile a genuine smile at your class and tell them it's nice to see them again (even if it isn't). Phrase negative feedback as constructively as you possibly can, and for every negative try to find two positives to state. Even if you feel they might be obvious ones, they might not be so obvious to the pupil. Little things like this will improve your rapport with your pupils and will encourage growth mindsets, emotional intelligence and an increasingly better relationship with the learning process.

1.8 Personalizing Learning

What exactly is personalized learning? It sounds superb. Christine Gilbert, the head of Ofsted for almost five years, describes personalized learning as:

> Taking a highly structured and responsive approach to each child's and young person's learning, in order that all are able to progress, achieve and participate. It means strengthening the link between learning and teaching by engaging pupils – and their parents – as partners in learning. (2007)

However, if we're being honest, it also sounds horrendous. What exactly is a highly structured and responsive approach in our classrooms? Why is it, around a decade since the term was first bandied about, that few teachers really jump up and down and shout out 'yes, yes, I love personalized learning. I know exactly what it is and I use it all the time'? I remember attending a Campaign for Learning event when the then Education Secretary, David Miliband, gave a keynote address about personalized learning. I was none the wiser by the end of it. Michael Gove's rhetoric is about old-fashioned values, but he seems a little vague as to what these actually are. Is personalized learning still on the agenda? In August 2011, the Department for Education doesn't seem to know. They seem a little preoccupied with cutting our budgets and our pensions.

My particular hope is that the good-quality ideas that came from the last few decades are retained, but without the needless paperwork, over-caution and general distrust of teachers to get it right. In a time of budget cuts and austerity measures, teachers' creativity will be the way to ensure that every child continues to receive a decent education and that each child they teach makes progress that is appropriate to that child, regardless of which party is in power.

Over time I've come to realize that personalized learning is actually a rather straightforward approach to learning in secondary schools. It's not actually about lots of paperwork, personalized learning plans (although these are useful and important for the right students), and stuff that's 'really only for primary schools'. It is really about knowing your students, some pre-emptive joined-up thinking and some good, creative, teaching.

Think about the range of pupils you teach. Are any of them in the following categories?

☐ Looked-after children

☐ Lower ability children

☐ Gifted children

☐ Talented children

☐ Children with a physical disability

☐ Children from a disadvantaged background

☐ Children with a specific educational need or needs

☐ Children that have fallen behind in their work for some reason, either known or unknown

☐ Children who haven't made the progress you think they ought to have

☐ Children from an ethnic background that statistically under-performs

☐ Children who seem withdrawn, perhaps bullied

☐ Children who you suspect might have a learning difficulty, but no one seems to have picked up on it

☐ Children whose parents are going through a divorce, or who have a difficult home situation that might end in something like divorce

☐ Children who have just had an argument with their family, friends or their boyfriend or girlfriend

☐ Children whose personal problems are getting in the way of their ability to focus in your lesson

There are so many circumstances, emotions and needs that you can never know all the issues going through the minds of your students. I always encourage my students to leave their problems at the classroom door, and set my classroom aside as somewhere that is a safe haven from all their worries. You can buy posters or make signs that say things like 'check you attitude at the door' and so on.

But this doesn't address every need your students have. In terms of their learning performance, different students need to focus on developing different skills and will make progress at slightly different rates. As I said earlier in the book, the 21st century requires the development of skills more than knowledge. Knowledge is important, but skills are the key to their future success. Therefore there are two straightforward ways to personalize learning: developing skills and assessing progress.

Developing Skills

One simple way to personalize learning is to focus on the skills that students should be able to develop during a unit of work. Students are exposed to a whole load of topics throughout their education, and many of the skills they will develop as a result of studying these topics are addressed by many different subjects. So it makes sense to ask students which skill they would like to focus on in this topic, and then to assess how well they developed in that skill.

Start a unit by identifying what knowledge and skills they should acquire and develop by the end of the unit. You might like to present students with a small handout, like the one below, and get them to pick from your list a skill that they will focus on. At the end of the unit, you and the student comment on how well they have developed that skill.

By the end of this unit you should have developed:

Knowledge	Skills
1.	1.
2.	2.
3.	3.
4.	4.
5.	5.
6.	6.
7.	7.

To be filled out at the start of the unit:

I am most interested in knowing:

The skill I would most like to develop is:

The beauty of this is that it empowers your pupils to take some control and responsibility over their learning, which is a key aspect of our next section – the Creative Classroom.

Assessing Progress

Assessing progress is most commonly known as Assessment for Learning (AfL). It is simply the process of observing the progress your students are making from one lesson to the next, and adapting your lessons to accommodate that progress. The Assessment Reform Group, set up in 2002, describes AfL as 'the process of seeking and interpreting evidence for use by learners and their teachers to decide where the learners are in their learning, where they need to go and how best to get there' (2002). This does not just mean marking their books after every lesson – although this is indeed a form of AfL – it means quick, observational, informal assessment. It could be their own self-assessment of their progress, or it could be peer-assessment and these should be added to your own assessment that informs your next steps.

To take our example from above, the AfL aspect is to get pupils to revisit, at set points in the unit, the skill that they have chosen to develop. A piece of homework could be designed to demonstrate that skill and you could mark it simply by commenting on how well they made progress in that skill. At the end of the unit you and the pupil could comment on a record sheet in a more summative way about their performance in that skill, and this could inform the pupil of what they need to do in the future to develop that skill further. I've given an example in the next section of the book.

Another example of AfL is to do with the lesson objectives you set. Having stated lesson objectives at the start of the lesson, you ask students to identify how well they have met those objectives. For instance, if the objective had been that *by the end of this lesson you will all know about X, most of you will know about Y and some of you will know about Z* then you ask for hands up who feels they know about X, Y and Z. Even better, you can ask students to give X, Y and Z a thumbs up if they are confident about that topic, a thumbs sideways if they are mostly okay with that topic and a thumbs down if they are unsure about that topic. So if their self-assessment revealed that not enough students know about X, then your next lesson needs to be adjusted. It may be that you need to be a bit more creative here about how to teach X, and take a different slant. We'll look at some structured ideas in the next section.

What if just one pupil had not met the success criteria you'd set for that lesson, or series of lessons? That's where the process has to get really personalized. What contextual factors might there be? Does the school's SENCO know, have you informed them, or the pupil's tutor? Can you sit down with the pupil and give them extra help, new targets, or direct them towards a peer mentor or another source of help? Moments such as this call for you to take action, and they bring to light the fact that not everyone operates according to your agenda.

The essence of AfL is that students become personally involved in the learning process, taking stock of where they are in their learning, what skills and habits they need to develop, and that they develop a growth mindset about making progress in their learning. This continuous cycle of input and reflection leads to a more creative and pupil-centred approach that can make your lessons suitably engaging and challenging for all your pupils.

1.9 In Summary

In order to be creative in the classroom you need to enter your creative state. It all comes down to knowledge and attitude. It is important to make sure that you understand the relevant educational theory properly; maybe even just reading this section has given you one or two ideas for doing something creative in your classroom. With your knowledge up to speed, check your attitude. How stressed are you? How motivated are you? How emotionally intelligent do you feel? Develop the ideas given here and look into others if you need to.

Whenever you come to school, or prepare work for school, then get into your creative state. Just tell yourself that you are feeling motivated, that you are fabulous at your job (of course) and think positively; visualize your lessons going smoothly and enjoyably. I have given you some tips for managing stress levels associated with teaching; make sure you try some of them out. As soon as you let negativity creep in, then thinking creatively is just not going to happen because you will start thinking of all the pitfalls that *could* happen. You would be horriblizing potentially excellent experiences for both you and your pupils. So start your teaching day positively; develop a mantra if you need to.

The other thing you must do is to employ some of the learning-styles information as soon as you can – even if you just make some notes about VAK and MI. Or, better still, analyse what you do at the moment to see where you are meeting learning styles suitably and where the areas are that you could develop. Ask yourself how you know that your pupils are making progress and think of the ways you can personalize their learning experience in your lessons. To help you, there is an audit exercise below. The sooner you start using the ideas in this book, the sooner you will feel more creative.

The best technique to enter your creative state is the simplest – be yourself. Or rather, be the best possible version of yourself you can be.

Being Creative Audit Exercise

Take a unit that you teach and use the table below to review its current and potential creativity. You can download copies of this table from the companion website.

Unit Title: _____ Year Group: _____

Lesson Topic	Knowledge to gain	Skills to gain		Teaching and Learning activities	VAK aspects	MI aspects	Personalized aspects	AfL aspects	Other Comments
			Current						
			Creative Alternative (if applicable)						
			Current						
			Creative Alternative (if applicable)						
			Current						
			Creative Alternative (if applicable)						

Chapter 2
The Creative Classroom

In this section:

2.1 What Do Pupils Need in Order to Learn Creatively?

- knowledge of how to learn and a sense of self-responsibility
- clear structure in their learning
- reasons to be interested in your subject
- a positive rapport with their teachers
- appropriate stimuli to keep the RAS alert
- positive and constructive feedback

2.2 What Teachers Need to Form a Creative Classroom

- a willingness to self-evaluate
- an ability to develop, or change, what you do presently
- accelerated learning techniques and structures incorporated into lessons
- knowledge of how to teach creatively

2.3 The Learning Process in the Creative Classroom

- clear structure in the lesson delivery
- connections that the pupils can make from one lesson to the next

- unit or topic success criteria

- ideas to get you started

- excellent planning

2.1 What do Pupils Need in Order to Learn Creatively?

So, we have looked at fundamental educational theory, and looked at how you can prepare your mindset in a positive way to approach creative teaching. But what about your pupils? What do they need, specifically?

I feel that in order to engage with creative learning and improve their learning performance, pupils need:

- knowledge of how to learn and a sense of self-responsibility

- clear structure in their learning

- reasons to be interested in your subject

- a positive rapport with their teachers

- appropriate stimuli to keep the RAS alert

- positive and constructive feedback

Why?

Knowledge of how to learn and a sense of self-responsibility

As stated in the last section, learning is not something that happens to a pupil. It is something in which they need to participate. Doing so can have a remarkable impact on a child's attitude not only to learning, but also to their life beyond and after school. Knowing how their brain works and what they can do to help themselves learn is the key to creative learning. They realize that there is an active role for them to play in their education, and they will become more involved in your lessons. This can be nurtured and a sense of personal responsibility and ownership over their learning can be developed. Doing this leads to all sorts of creative possibilities in their learning, but at a fundamental level it gets them on your side and interested in learning.

Clear structure in their learning

It is no good appealing to pupils' right brain and getting all creative, if you don't level that out with structure from the left brain. Information is inherently logical, but it can be presented as a series of unconnected ideas. Teachers need to ensure that they are being as logical as possible, organizing information in a clear structure to make sure it makes sense. Likewise, pupils need to have a sense of how their learning activities at one moment fit in with other learning activities. They need to see a 'big picture' of the information they are learning. So creative teaching requires a systematic approach to learning.

Similarly, if pupils perceive your creative lessons as a series of daft games with little or no relevance to anything they are learning, then the whole process becomes pointless, and probably rather rowdy too. Pupils need to understand why they are doing what they are doing, and the consequences of not following instructions. For example, can you trust your pupils to discuss something in pairs without starting to chat about last night's TV instead? A strong discipline structure based on trust and personal responsibility on the part of the pupil forms the backbone of any successful creative classroom. See 'A note about discipline' (below) for more about creative environments and discipline.

FACT BOX – *A NOTE ABOUT DISCIPLINE*

This is a tricky one. You need to give pupils enough leeway to express themselves creatively, but maintain enough control to make sure that pupils don't abuse this level of freedom. 'Strict and scary' styles of teaching don't lend themselves to a successful creative environment, but neither does the Joyce Grenfell approach (George, don't do that ...). It's about mixing approachability and authority, being clear about what you want, being fair and having high expectations. There are plenty of good books out there about discipline, so I won't attempt a thorough investigation of it here as I won't be able to do it justice. Suffice it to say that you need to have clear ground-rules about attempts to sabotage an activity or failing to participate. When warning a pupil about their behaviour, you need to be clear about *why* the pupil's behaviour is wrong, how they should remedy the situation and what consequences they may face if their behaviour remains unacceptable. You need to be firm and consistent without being confrontational or aggressive. Most or all your complaint is directed towards the pupil's behaviour, not their personality, and the consequence is a result of their behaviour, not a punishment from you. This way you de-personalize the error and the sanction, meaning that neither you nor the pupil needs to lose face.

Reasons to be interested in your subject

A very natural question that pupils ask themselves about anything they learn is 'What's in it for me?' The standard carrot of good exam grades is often not a satisfactory answer to this question. Pupils want to know why they should bother learning the things you have to teach them – what intrinsic value do they have? What relevance does this lesson have in the grand scheme of life?

If a pupil is naturally motivated by your subject, then the intrinsic value of anything you teach them is obvious: they like your subject, want to know more and want to get better at it. But if they are not naturally interested in your subject, then the intrinsic value is less obvious. A pupil's RAS may not engage with your lessons and any work you give them, however creative you might make it, is 'pointless' or 'a waste of time'.

Often there are key skills to be gained from learning about a particular topic, or participating in a particular learning activity, and it is this kind of thing you need to emphasize to such pupils. If you can find ways of relating what you are teaching to something they are already familiar with in their own lives, that can be a very powerful way in to pupils' interest. For instance, in modern foreign languages, you could show extracts from episodes of *Friends* or *The Simpsons* in your target language – they are available on DVD from the Amazon website of your target language's country. You might make a link just by being able to say 'It's kind of like when ...' and relating what you are learning about to something that they would have experienced before in real life or in a film or on television. Knowledge and understanding is, after all, based on associations you make between things you already know and the things you learn. If there isn't something familiar for your pupils to link new information to, then it loses context for them and is far harder to memorize or understand.

A positive rapport with their teachers

This ties together the last three points. The rapport a teacher has with his or her pupils can make a huge difference; and it can largely be controlled by the teacher. Do they feel comfortable with you? The respect they have for you: is it out of fear or genuine respect for you and what you stand for? A positive attitude from the teacher makes a big difference to pupil motivation, behaviour and performance. But the teacher's attitude should also be conditional. The teacher should be very clear about the rules and what is and isn't acceptable and should take steps to demonstrate to pupils that misbehaviour (which includes a lack of effort or participation) is unacceptable.

The effect of making pupils feel valued (such as knowing their names, and something of their personality) cannot be underestimated. *Even if the teacher doesn't actually remember everybody's names, or care too much about the individual – or even like them!* The trick here is to make pupils feel as if what they are learning is important and relevant (so they understand why they are learning it), and make them care about the work – to get them feeling involved in the learning process. Once this is established, pupils will become more autonomous as they get older, and will be much more likely to enjoy learning for the sake of learning.

A teacher who does not appear to value or respect his or her pupils is unlikely to elicit such positive progress. However, if this is your teaching style (you're a 'strict and scary' teacher) and you wish to change tactics, then please don't just walk into class and act differently, valuing your pupils and being all positive and friendly. The pupils will think you've flipped and it won't work. I've included in the next section some incremental steps to take that might work for you.

Appropriate stimuli to keep the RAS alert

Telling jokes, making the pupils feel welcome, using artefacts, questioning pupils, through to doing something more unusual like re-enactments, making models, or even just getting pupils to bob up in their seats instead of putting their hands up. These are all examples of creative stimuli that get pupils' attention.

Often creative teaching taps into the various learning styles models. Phil Beadle, 2004's Teacher of the Year, often sang silly songs to his pupils to tap into their musical intelligence. Maybe that's not what you're good at doing, but it is a legitimate example of creative stimuli that involve pupils in learning.

Positive and constructive feedback

How would you like it if at the end of a rather good lesson of yours, your pupils came up to you and said 'Very good work, but you need to pay more attention to the accuracy of your delivery. You did not ask Jack to answer any of your questions, even though his hand was up more often than not. You also failed to enquire how your pupils were at the start of the lesson and state the lesson objectives clearly. However, we did enjoy your lesson and we'll look forward to an even better one next time.'

Imagine that you worked hard to prepare that lesson. You spent a lot of energy and care over getting it right, and you were happy that you had produced a very good lesson. Comments like the one above focus too heavily on what went wrong, and not enough on what went right and what to do about the things that went wrong. They are deflating despite the positive comments.

How many of us teachers are guilty of taking a good piece of work and spending more time criticizing it negatively than positively, contaminating the praise with a somewhat disproportionate list of errors without a similar list of good points? Creative teachers are meant to educate and inspire their pupils, not bombard them with a list of their failings with no constructive help on how to improve.

You and I know that marking and giving feedback involves looking for progress and development in their work, but in the context of my example above does it not seem a little terse? At least the pupils in my example gave prompt feedback; in our modern world of computer games and mobile phones, most feedback young people experience is fairly instant. In the classroom, for legitimate reasons, feedback can take a week (or more) to reach the pupil. Not terribly twenty-first-century, is it?

As a teacher you need to look at the simplest solution to giving effective feedback. One simple piece of advice is to write/say 'and' wherever you might normally use 'but' to stop the 'negative' outweighing the positives. Another is to force yourself into a ratio of two positive comments to one constructive comment.

To speed things up, you could simply get pupils to identify their own targets and get them to do a self-assessment or peer-assessment about how effectively they met their targets. This could be an initial exercise prior to your final marking (which could focus solely on their targets if you wish) but at least there's some prompt feedback, and you are encouraging self-reflection which is an important tool that encourages and enables independent learning.

This is also the benefit of AfL – quick feedback between you and your pupils that's focussed on positive progress.

2.2 What Teachers Need to Form a Creative Classroom

Getting into your creative state is very important. But there is a little more to it than just positive thinking and some knowledge about educational theory. Here are a few more things to consider:

- your willingness to self-evaluate

- your ability to develop, or change, what you do presently

- incorporating accelerated learning techniques and structures into lessons

- knowledge of how to teach creatively

Willingness to self-evaluate

If you don't review what you do, then how can you ever assess if you can do better? Every job involves some self-evaluation, and teaching is no different. You probably do it quite naturally in your head – deciding if a lesson went well or not, and why, for example. But what about you as a teacher overall? When was the last time you reflected about how you conduct yourself as a teacher?

As you have read this far into the book, you are most probably willing and open-minded enough to do a little self-evaluation. You need to reflect on what you are doing at present to work out what you already do well, and what you might need to improve on or do differently. There is also some groundwork to be done in order to ensure that your classroom environment facilitates and encourages creativity. Use the classroom audit in the next fact box to assess how conducive your classroom environment is to a creative atmosphere.

FACT BOX – CLASSROOM AUDIT

The environment can have a very significant effect on pupils and staff alike. How someone feels about the environment around them has implications for how they behave in that environment. Take a look at the classroom you are in now and consider these points:

Outside the classroom

What is there around the door to the classroom to make the room inviting?

_____

_____

Describe the displays (if any) in the vicinity of the classroom.

_____

_____

How old do they appear to be?

_____

Inside the classroom –

Displays

Describe the displays (if any) in the classroom.

_____

_____

Are the walls used effectively to encourage
interest in the subject? For example: are there
puzzles, things to debate, something interactive
to use in a lesson, something to aid reviewing,
something to promote the subject/topic?   Yes/No
Why? _____

_____

There are plants in the room   Yes/No
The classroom is tidy and well organized   Yes/No

The room is a pleasant environment to be in   Yes/No
What could you, the teacher, do to improve the
environment of this classroom?

_____

_____

Maintenance
The walls and ceiling are clean and well painted   Yes/No
The tables are in good condition overall   Yes/No
The chairs are in good condition overall   Yes/No
The teacher's desk and chair is in good condition Yes/No
The floors are carpeted   Yes/No
The classroom is tidy   Yes/No
The room is well ventilated   Yes/No
There are good-quality curtains or blinds at the
windows   Yes/No
All the lights work   Yes/No
What could the school do to improve the environment of
this classroom?

_____

_____

Equipment

There is a computer in the room   Yes/No
It shows signs of being used by the teacher   Yes/No
It is gathering dust   Yes/No
It is linked to a projector or interactive whiteboard Yes/No
The chalkboard/whiteboard is in good condition   Yes/No
Any comments about the standard of equipment present, its
use and/or any equipment that may be required in the room.

_____

Your evaluation about this classroom
In your opinion, how welcoming is it, and what makes it an
interesting room to be in?

In your opinion, what additions or changes would this classroom benefit from?

Other thoughts

Looking at the previous chapter, we can divide pupils' needs into rapport, structure and creativity. Below is a checklist of things *not* to be doing as far as rapport, structure and creativity are concerned. Tick all the ones you find yourself doing. Be honest!

Rapport

☐ Underestimating pupils' capabilities

☐ Communicating negative expectations

☐ Comparing pupils

☐ Having favourites

☐ Shouting a lot at your pupils

☐ Making pupils prove themselves

☐ Using ability as a way to measure self-worth

☐ Suggesting to pupils that ability is fixed

☐ Showing no interest in pupils

☐ You do not know pupils' names

☐ You do not know pupils' special educational needs

☐ You show active dislike or contempt for some pupils

☐ You show active dislike or contempt for a whole class (or classes)

☐ Not keeping promises

☐ Failing to admit your mistakes

☐ Not listening to your pupils

☐ Dismissing pupils' suggestions

☐ Using fear motivation, or intimidation

Structure

☐ You act as if you are superior

☐ You control for the sake of controlling, not for the sake of learning

☐ You do not explain to pupils what to do, you tell

☐ You impose oppressive rules that go beyond the school's rules

☐ You apply rules inconsistently

☐ You use empty threats/don't follow through on punishments you threaten

☐ You don't follow the rules

☐ You degrade or intimidate pupils

☐ You create uncertainty by not making clear what outcomes are expected

Creativity

☐ You set unattainable goals

☐ You create uncertainty through vague outcomes

☐ You show a lack of enthusiasm for what you are teaching

☐ You fail to explain the purpose and/or relevance of the material being covered

☐ There is little enjoyment of learning in your classroom

☐ Most learning exercises involve writing large amounts of text with pupils working by themselves

☐ There is a lack of pace

☐ Pupils seem bored in your lessons

☐ Pupils who misbehave claim that they are bored

☐ Your worksheets are mostly fill-in-the-gap exercises

☐ You do pupils' work for them

Ability to develop, or change, what you do presently

Think of when you last shouted at a class or at a pupil: did you choose to shout, or did you just lose your temper? Teaching is an act. No matter what kind of learning environment you have, pupils will misbehave. It is entirely natural that when you put 20 to 30 children together in one room they will not all get on with each other, with you or their work the entire time. A creative classroom environment might do more to engage pupils who misbehave, but the reasons for their behaviour are complex and not entirely under your control by any means.

My point here is that there needs to be a level of professional detachment on your part that analyses how you conduct yourself in your classroom. Have you smiled at the class? Did you remember to welcome them, tell them it was nice to see them again and then recap the previous lesson? What strategies do you have in place to deal with certain pupils in your class? What possibilities have you mentally prepared yourself for in terms of pupil behaviour? How will you deal with any attempts to sabotage your lesson (see fact box on sabotage below)? What funny things or interesting facts could you tell them? How does what they are learning today fit in with everything else they are doing, and what does it relate to that they might find familiar? What personal issues do you have, and can you make sure that these do not affect your attitude to your class?

If you have the ability to look at how you act in front of your pupils, and then amend your actions as necessary, you are more than halfway there. Teaching has to be something of an act, a performance, because otherwise you are just being too honest with your pupils. You leave yourself open to feeling upset and personally offended by pupils who are rude or don't work sufficiently well for you. Because they are children, they are not fully in control of their feelings and emotions and will play up. Many badly behaved children at school grow up to regret the way they acted.

Unlike your pupils, you are in control of your feelings (think emotional intelligence) so why stress yourself out shouting at them or simply feeling depressed by their behaviour when you can act and react to them using your head instead? This means, for example, that if you shout, you've chosen to shout because you felt it was the most appropriate thing to do, not because you were getting angry. Such a judicious approach will most probably reduce the frequency with which you shout, and as such will make pupils take you far more seriously when or, preferably, if you do raise your voice. You are perfectly able to change the way you choose to perform in the classroom: just think back to the discussion of mindsets in the previous section.

FACT BOX – SABOTAGE

How do you handle attempts to sabotage your lesson? Pupils with behavioural issues will try to do things to draw attention to themselves or, apparently, simply to annoy you! There are many reasons for this kind of behaviour which I don't need to discuss here, but you must not permit it because you leave yourself open to all sorts of problems and you are not doing your bit to ensure that such pupils become responsible citizens.

Nor can you simply tell them off or get angry with them; it may or may not deal with the current situation but it will do little to discourage future attempts at sabotaging your lessons. It is also not a very positive way to deal with it; you'll be reducing that pupil's dignity and can reduce your approachability in the eyes of that pupil and other pupils.

Remember that you cannot control pupils' behaviour, you can only influence it. So if a pupil misbehaves, it isn't likely to be your fault – it is the choice of the pupil to misbehave.

First you should remain calm within yourself. Will a joke or a (non-sarcastic) witticism alleviate the situation? If it is more serious, explain the situation to the pupil – preferably one-to-one rather than in front of the whole class – and

---

explain why the pupil's behaviour is wrong, or why they need to do the given activity. Explaining why is always a good tactic (provided that there is a good reason 'why') as it allows you to justify why you are correct and the pupil is not correct without placing personal blame on the pupil. It is also wise to explain what the logical consequence will be if their current behaviour continues. It de-personalizes things somewhat, removing the suggestion that you dislike the pupil. It is just their behaviour you dislike.

You could also have something of a points system. It could be personalized, or it could relate to a school-wide house points system for example. Personally, I like the idea of dividing the class up into teams – maybe ones relevant to the topic you are studying – and awarding points to that team for good work, good contribution to activities in class, and so on, while deducting points for bad behaviour or a lack of effort. A little bit of peer pressure should keep pupils behaving, especially if there is a good prize to be won. It doesn't have to be a money-based prize; it could be chocolate or (better still) the opportunity to do something such as perform in front of the class, or teach on a subject of their choice, for example.

Earlier I mentioned using the word 'and' instead of 'but' when giving pupils feedback. This is another example of using your head when teaching. By being aware of how you say things, you can do a lot to ensure a positive reaction from pupils, fostering a positive rapport and ultimately a more creative, secure learning environment.

Using accelerated learning

My company, Learning Performance, has been teaching accelerated learning techniques in schools since 1994. There are two parts to it: learning skills (or study skills) that the pupils should use, and a model for the learning process that teachers should use with their pupils' active involvement. We will look at the learning process in chapter 2 section 3.

Study Skills refer to a range of activities and techniques that pupils can use to make learning easier. To clarify, 'learning' in this instance means anything that has to be memorized and understood. So study skills are memory techniques, understanding and summarizing techniques and revision techniques. All three categories can be used in your creative teaching, but it will be the understanding techniques you will probably focus on most in class time.

Memory techniques come in two varieties. The variety that deals with memorizing those tricky little details and the variety that deals with memorizing whole topics of work or other major concepts. The most popular and familiar memory technique for little details is a mnemonic. This can, for instance, be where you take the first letter of each of the words to be recalled and use them to make up a silly sentence using the letters to start new words. So, for instance, in order to memorize both the names of the planets (Mercury, Venus, Earth, Mars, Jupiter, Saturn, Uranus, Neptune and Pluto) and the order they come in, you could say to yourself: *My Very Easy Method Just Speeds Up Naming Planets*, or more amusingly *My Very Energetic Mother Just Swam Under the North Pole*. The point of this technique is not to create another layer of things for the pupil to remember, but to create *triggers* that aid the pupil's learning. So the word 'planets' becomes associated with the silly mnemonic (which appeals to all sorts of imagination areas of the brain) and the first letters trigger the original words learnt.

Other similar techniques include peg words and image chains. A peg word is a word that rhymes with a number and can be easily visualized. You then get pupils to 'hook' each word to be memorized on a peg word. So, for instance, with a list of ten words you would get pupils to visualize the first thing on their list melting in the sun (because sun rhymes with one), or some other imaginative association they can make between the item and the peg word. Two's peg word could be shoe, three – tree, and so on. The reason for using a peg word is that numbers are not particularly tangible in the imagination, but a word easily associable with each is. You can have a lot of fun getting pupils to remember the list words at random, ask them for number seven on their list and I guarantee you it will trigger near-instant recall. Note that this is not about understanding, this is about remembering key words.

An image chain is a similar idea, but can be used quite a bit more flexibly than other memory techniques. Pupils need to use their imagination to visualize a series of images that depict the things they have to memorize. Think of it as being like a movie, a comic or a storyboard in their minds. Less tangible words that are hard to imagine can be substituted using the same first letter or a word that rhymes. Events in the story they will create will trigger the words they need to recall.

Study skills that are effective in dealing with whole topics or other coherent 'chunks' of information involve making sure that pupils understand the work fully too. By 'understanding' I am not only referring to whether or not a pupil 'gets it' but whether they can spot how information is interconnected, and how well they can break information down to its relevant component parts.

All information is organized. There is the overall theme, the main ideas – which act like chapter headings – and then the primary details which tend to give the who, what, why, when, where and how about the main ideas, and then the secondary (and tertiary, and so on) details which expand upon the primary details with examples, exceptions and the like. How many of your GCSE and A-level pupils could take a unit they have just been studying and break it down like this? The thing is, in order for them to be able to answer top-level exam questions sufficiently well this is the skill that is required. If they understand the topic, they will be able to pick out the relevant parts to talk about and allude to all the right connected ideas.

The best way to combine both understanding and memorizing is to get pupils to map out topics or chunks. Maps are creative and logical diagrams that organize thoughts and help to formulate the structure of the information to be memorized. By using colour and images and by forcing the mind to be logical, mapping combines both right and left brain very effectively and engages most people's RAS. There are some guidelines to getting this technique right. First, maps are not brainstorms or spider diagrams; words and images should be written or drawn directly onto the lines, not in bubbles floating off somewhere else. This helps the mind associate and recall things in the right place. Second, less is more. Keywords, not sentences, should go on the map. This is not the place for masses of detail; triggers should be used instead. Here's an outline of what a good map could look like:

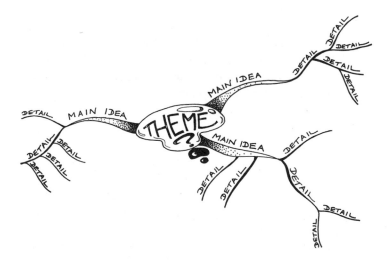

It is not restricted to just two or three main branches, but I would not recommend more than six because then it becomes rather cluttered. The reason this technique works is because the pupils have been actively involved in making the map, quite independent of you, the teacher. So do not make maps for your pupils, but let them make the maps themselves. You might, of course, like to point them in the right direction with things to include on the map!

The last study skill to look at is revision. It always amazed us at Learning Performance how few pupils know how to do this properly, and how few schools do a lot to help them with this. It is ironic that the one aspect of the learning process that pupils have complete control over is the one they find most boring. But the boredom is somewhat unnecessary, as are the numerous tortuous hours spent revising – or rather cramming – in the run-up to the exams. Pupils, and teachers, often get revision and relearning mixed up. If pupils look at their notes, do not recall what the information is about and then start breaking the information down into its component parts, that is not revision. Revision is when pupils look at their notes, recognize the information and can recall it, test themselves and compare it with their original notes, spot their successes and identify areas to be relearned or reinforced. Surely the word 'revision' means 'to look again'? Not 'to learn again'.

Creative teachers can help pupils revise by giving them first summary exercises to do for homework, such as a mapping exercise, and then doing recall tests in class. These tests do not have to be strict exam-style tests (although there is a place for doing so); it could simply be redrawing maps, or playing games such as Trivial Pursuit but with questions on your subject – the pupils could have prepared the questions themselves, or you can purchase memory flashcards which should be suitable.

Knowledge of how to teach creatively: the philosophy of the creative classroom

The creative classroom enhances learning in two ways: it makes learning more enjoyable, and it enables pupils to produce better work. The philosophy of the creative classroom, as expounded by Peter Kline (1997) is that *learning is most effective when it is fun*. By *fun* I do not mean that you need to be funnier than Lee Evans and more inventive than Johnny Ball. And there are topics that are simply not meant to be 'fun', that are in fact very serious. By *fun* Peter Kline really means that you are not going to learn very effectively if you are passive and/or bored.

How can you take what you do at the moment and make it better? For instance, I once had to teach my GCSE Religious Studies class about how the Sunni/Shia split came about in Islam. To be honest with you, it wasn't going to be a particularly good lesson. The split occurred simply because some of the followers of Muhammad couldn't agree on who should be their new leader. Pupils have to learn the names of the main players and how they relate to each other. We were reading from the textbook, and pupils were simply going to write answers to the questions in the book. Nothing wrong with that, but they were not going to be particularly interested in the exercise (they were a very kinaesthetic group) and, as such, they would probably not remember the topic so easily – or at best resent having to revise, or relearn, it later on.

As we were reading through the text, one pupil said, 'I'm getting really confused!' and others chimed in agreement. No big surprise. So I suggested that we make a diagram on the board. It's a class of 16 pupils, so it wasn't hard to gather them around and get them to take it in turns to write up the next name on the board and doodle important information next to names, and so on. The pupils understood it all much better when they had all participated in discovering the information for themselves (well, ok, with a little help from me) and mapped it out as a team. Moreover, they enjoyed themselves. Then they quickly copied it down, answering many of the questions in the textbook, but in a diagram instead. They had all been actively engaged, no one had been allowed to be passive, they had worked collaboratively and I had facilitated their learning without spoon-feeding. I had enjoyed myself more, they had enjoyed themselves more and had actually learned the material far more effectively and efficiently than they may have done otherwise. Everyone was a winner.

It's not much of a stretch of an idea to get the pupils to make the diagram physically, with each pupil (or a group of pupils) representing a key person or piece of information in this story. It would make for a good review exercise.

If pupils are engaged, interested and enjoying themselves, then it is important to make sure the structure is there for them to improve their learning performance. There needs to be an improvement in standards of work and grades to make this all worthwhile. And, of course, when I set a piece of written work about the split, my pupils wrote excellent work that showed a clear understanding of what took place and the ramifications it had for Islam. They applied what they had learned to the questions asked without any real direct input from me and they succeeded. Even those who were struggling in my subject and elsewhere performed well in this assignment. It goes to show that once motivated, and when taking responsibility for their own learning, there is a lot a pupil can achieve.

So, taking everything thus far in this book into account, we can say that the philosophy of the creative classroom is this: creativity with a healthy dose of independent learning is the key to making learning more effective.

So step 1 to achieve our philosophy is to ensure that the pupils feel secure with you and in your environment. This will allow and enable creativity. Step 2 is to make sure all your pupils feel valued. This will encourage confidence and positive participation in your lessons. You don't want a two-tier classroom set-up, where some pupils become stars at this kind of thing and the others become passive observers. Step 3 is to encourage feelings of personal responsibility for their work and to empower pupils to be more autonomous so that their learning performance, including their ability to learn for themselves, improves.

Here's a breakdown of those three steps, and some self-evaluation opportunities for you to consider where you are at in each step and what you might like to do to develop each step.

Step 1: Security

Pupils need to have the freedom to be themselves, and the coherent structure to prevent utter anarchy. This is the most fundamental thing to cater for when establishing a creative classroom.

Creativity is an expression of the self, so if pupils cannot be themselves in your classroom, then their creativity will be inhibited for fear of judgement from you or from their peers. However, there needs to be a clear framework for learning in your classroom too. Freedom to be themselves does not equate with freedom not to work or freedom to annoy other pupils and their teacher!

Pupils need to come into your classroom knowing that they will be safe – that they are highly unlikely to be made a fool of (by their peers or their teacher), to worry, to feel stupid, to feel unappreciated or unwanted and to leave unrewarded for their effort. Instead they will come to expect your classroom to be a place where they feel welcomed, their opinions are valued, they learn and develop, and they know what the rules are, understand them and are willing to follow them.

Using our three headings from earlier – rapport, structure and creativity – use the checklist below to consider what you do already to encourage a sense of security among pupils in your classroom. Then pick something from each list that you could try out in your classroom.

Rapport

☐ You communicate positive expectations

☐ You show that you want to get to know pupils

☐ You can greet pupils by name

☐ You express tasks as learning processes, not evaluations

☐ You emphasize the importance of putting in effort, rather than the importance of ability

☐ You actively demonstrate an interest in and enjoyment of teaching

☐ You actively demonstrate an enjoyment of your subject

☐ You realize when a pupil is not feeling well

Structure

☐ You set limits without being oppressive or over-controlling

☐ You emphasize the goals and the purpose of learning

☐ You communicate and explain rules and routines clearly

☐ You apply rules, routines and penalties consistently

☐ You apply penalties because of the pupil's behaviour, not because of the pupil's character

☐ You express rules in terms of appropriate, rather than prohibited, behaviour

☐ You have authority and can exercise control

☐ You make clear expected outcomes

☐ Pupils will know what to expect in your lessons when it comes to behaviour and routine

Creativity

☐ You show enthusiasm for your subject

☐ You explain why

☐ You set appropriate, attainable goals

☐ You highlight the importance/usefulness of the work

☐ You give clear instructions and objectives

☐ You increase pupils' knowledge and understanding

☐ You try to make lessons enjoyable and stimulating

☐ You use differentiated materials when appropriate

☐ You take the lead; you are the expert, informing learners

☐ You use a range of learning activities

Step 2: Being valued

In addition to enabling pupils to be themselves, the next thing you need to foster in your pupils is a sense of intrinsic worth. As we considered in the last section, children and teenagers can be emotionally insecure, so while you might be able to look after issues of external security, you need to draw out pupils' creative nature. In younger children creativity is often not a difficulty, but teenagers frequently doubt their own abilities in this area (as well as in others). If you appear to value pupils' input, praise their positive contributions to your lessons, and combine this with the secure environment you create in your classroom, then pupils will be more motivated and respond more enthusiastically and effectively to your lessons.

As with the previous checklist, tick the things you already do to make pupils feel valued and pick one thing from each list that you could try to do.

Rapport

☐ You know your pupils' characters

☐ You create a non-judgemental environment in your classroom

☐ You emphasize, and appreciate, what each pupil is good at

☐ You encourage pupils to develop their interests rather than please you

☐ You encourage pupils to improve themselves rather than prove themselves

☐ You believe, and make clear this belief to your pupils, that if you believe you can, or believe you can't, then you're right

☐ You focus on individual progress and achievement, rather than comparison

☐ You encourage pupils to ask questions and express their opinions

☐ You always remind pupils how much they are learning

☐ You show your pupils the many ways to be successful

☐ You admit, and apologize, if you are wrong

☐ You ask your pupils for feedback about their experience of learning in your lessons

Structure

☐ Although you make pupils accountable, you try not to use your authority in an imposing manner

☐ You help pupils to set realistic goals for themselves

☐ You encourage pupils to use sensible self-control, rather than giving them lots of petty instructions

☐ You recognize that pupils have feelings

☐ You don't take yourself too seriously and exercise a sense of humour

☐ Your pupils willingly agree to rules and learning objectives

Creativity

☐ You try to create curiosity through variety

☐ You encourage pupils to use their creative side

☐ You adapt teaching methods to pupils' learning styles

☐ You allow pupils to perform to the limits of their ability, and you set them challenges to push their ability further

☐ You engage pupils through activities like problem-solving, role-play and simulation

☐ Pupils have a sense that the work being completed is relevant and meaningful

☐ You relate the curriculum to pupils' own lives and experiences

☐ You use what pupils are interested in and think is relevant in your lessons

☐ You emphasize the learning process

☐ You use kinaesthetic activities in your lessons

☐ You expect positivity and participation from pupils

Stage 3: Independent learning

One of the biggest changes that took place in the twentieth century was the nature of the workplace. So many companies today expect their employees to be able to learn new skills whenever necessary. It could be argued that the outcomes of schooling are now more focused on transferable skills than on academic knowledge, reflecting the relentless march of the information age: what you were able to do yesterday may be out of date by tomorrow.

Moreover, if pupils feel they have an element of control and input into their learning, they will participate far more effectively in the process of learning. By control I don't mean that they dictate the agenda – you know best; as teacher you are still the expert. Instead I mean their ability to evaluate their own progress, to spot for themselves the skills they can learn from an activity, and to be entrusted not to go off-task when asked to discuss something with their neighbour. This is obviously something which requires a degree of maturity, and full autonomy would be something I would expect from A-level pupils, but for it to work without great upheaval at that age, it can be encouraged in younger pupils, from around the age of ten in Years 6 and 7 (P7 and S1 in Scotland).

 As before, tick the things you currently find yourself doing and highlight something from each list you think you might like to try.

Rapport

☐ You encourage pupils to give positive feedback to each other

☐ You ask your pupils about what helps them to learn best, and respond appropriately

☐ You accept feedback from pupils neutrally and calmly

☐ Pupils in your class are confident that you know them and understand them well

☐ Pupils in your class are confident that they must all participate, and are motivated to do so

Structure

☐ The focus is on learning, not on you

☐ You encourage pupil autonomy by giving pupils leadership roles, choices, a share of responsibilities and opportunities for decision-making

☐ You help pupils to develop skills that enable them to take responsibility for their learning and solve their own problems

☐ You allow pupils to set their own schedules, choose their own work methods, the order in which they will work on tasks, take breaks, etc.

Creativity

☐ You enable pupils to learn things for themselves: there is a feeling of discovery in your lessons

☐ You help pupils set realistic goals for themselves

☐ You model the attitudes you expect from pupils, such as patience, persistence and learning from mistakes

☐ You help pupils to create their own ways of learning something

☐ You encourage pupils to reorganize and review their notes

These checklists contain a series of ideas and attitudes that you can employ in your teaching to facilitate the development of your creative classroom environment. Getting creative teaching right is far more about what you think and how you act upon those thoughts, rather than simply employing a range of fancy teaching tricks.

If you just start introducing creative learning activities without much regard for the context in which they should be conducted, then you run the risk of everything falling flat. Without the right rapport in place, pupils won't appreciate the effort you've gone to, or the purpose of the activity. If pupils don't feel safe and valued with you, then they may be reluctant to participate effectively, or underestimate their ability to do the activity. Without a good discipline structure in place, pupils may sabotage your activity, and use the unusual level of autonomy you've granted them to disrupt others' learning, bully and/or undermine your authority and confidence.

Hopefully you've identified a lot of things that you already do to foster creativity, and can identify some other things you could try to do. With these in place, you should feel free to experiment with some of the ideas to get you started in the next chapter. You should feel free and confident to come up with your own ideas – my ideas are just a trigger to get you thinking.

2.3 The Learning Process in the Creative Classroom

So now all the theory and self-evaluation is over, let's organize what all this means and make it practical and applicable to your teaching. The learning process in the creative classroom needs:

- clear structure in the lesson delivery

- connections that the pupils can make from one lesson to the next

- unit or topic success criteria

- ideas to get you started that engage pupils with your lesson content, with you and with your subject in general

- excellent planning from you, the teacher, to bring all this together

Clear structure in the lesson delivery

This is all down to expectations. What do your pupils expect when they come into your classroom? Will you be prepared for them? Will the start of the lesson be formal or informal? Will they understand what it is you want them to do, or will they have to ask? Will you engage with them throughout the lesson, or will you have a sneaky peak at your emails at some point? Or, as one pupil informed me recently about a colleague, will you be booking your holiday instead of teaching them? Will you finish on time, or in a hurry? Patterns of your behaviour, which reflect many things about you, are picked up on pretty quickly by your pupils. If you want to avoid behavioural issues when it comes to providing them with more active and creative tasks, then you have to make sure that their expectations are right and your lessons are well structured.

Does your department have a vision statement? Is it on display in your classroom? Does your school have rules for the classroom? Are they on display too? Ideally you need something that you can defer to, something on the walls that essentially says to the pupils, 'this is what you are here for and this is what you will do'. I would just set a few simple ground rules if your school does not have a policy of displaying common rules in classrooms: stand in silence at the start and end of lessons and wait for the teacher to start the lesson before sitting down; if the teacher or another pupil is speaking, show them respect and listen to them without talking; do as the teacher directs you to do; maintain a learning ethos throughout the lesson.

The last two rules give you quite a lot of professional flexibility. The first one, about silence at the start and end, sounds terribly old fashioned I know – but it really does work. By having a formal start to the lesson, pupils can take a moment to pause, take themselves away from whatever other thoughts they had and focus on your lesson. Likewise, by having a formal ending pupils leave your lesson sensibly and it gives you the opportunity to share a final reflection on the lesson with them. It might be hard to establish these rules totally by yourself, so perhaps you could bring this up at a department meeting to get support from your colleagues. If you all do it, it becomes the norm for pupils.

Lessons themselves should follow a clear pattern. When you write an essay, it has three parts:

1   an introduction that gives the context, states your objectives and highlights what is coming

2   the main body of the text

3   and a conclusion that sums up what the essay said

In fact, most things that convey information follow this sort of tripartite pattern. And so should your lessons.

There should be a clear introduction, or starter, that should:

- help pupils understand the context of the lesson,

- give them an idea of what to expect,

- provide some objectives/success criteria that they can judge themselves by

The middle of the lesson should:

- contain a range of activities that pupils can engage with

- contain opportunities for pupils to collaborate with others and to work alone

- contain opportunities for pupils to discover something for themselves – some teachers refer to this as 'The

Pit', a part of a lesson where pupils really have to work (collaboratively or individually) to find out the answers for themselves

Likewise the conclusion, or plenary, of the lesson should give:

- pupils the opportunity to reiterate and sum up what they have learned so as to reinforce it for their own benefit

- you the opportunity to see how well pupils have learned – to assess the learning – so as to judge the success of the lesson and plan ahead

While creative teaching must follow this clear structure in order to make sure that meaningful learning takes place, it should be pointed out that the structure shouldn't be too rigid, otherwise it will cause you too many difficulties. In some lessons you won't want to state overt success criteria at the start because it might give the game away, especially if your pupils will be entering the pit. One very simple example of some flexible success criteria that will help with your assessment for learning would be to have a PowerPoint slide at the start of the lesson that simply stated 'By the end of this lesson you all should be able to [...], most of you could be able to [...] and some of you might be able to [...]' and at the end of the lesson, you show the slide again and take a show of hands as to who has achieved one or more of your success criteria. You could keep this focussed on skills rather than knowledge, or it could be differentiated by quantity.

To give some examples, your success criteria could be:

By the end of this lesson:

- you all should be able to name **ten** elements from the periodic table,

- most of you could be able to name **fifteen**, and

- some of you might be able to name **twenty** or more.

Or your success criteria could be:

By the end of this lesson:

- you all should be able to **discuss** the importance of the Gandhi's teaching on non-violence,

- most of you could be able to **analyse and evaluate** his teaching on non-violence, and

- some of you might be able to **state and justify your point of view** about non-violence.

And you don't simply have to ask for a show of hands for each part of the criteria, you could ask for a 'fist of five' at each point. A fist of five is where pupils rate from naught to five how confident they are with whatever you ask of them using the fingers on their fist. You'll find that pupils tend to be brutally honest about this sort of thing, especially if they know that they could be asked to prove it! There are more ideas on these sort of starters and plenaries in the next chapter.

Connections that the pupils can make from one lesson to the next

Slightly more advanced than simply setting success criteria is to incorporate an activity like the Learning Pyramid. Having established the lesson's success criteria, you get pupils to draw a rough triangle and divide it horizontally into three sections, or you could make a template to distribute to everyone. In the bottom section pupils are asked to write what they already know about the lesson's topic. This is an excellent starter activity, especially following straight on from stating the success criteria, as it requires pupils to think back to previous lessons – or learning from elsewhere – so they are making strong connections in their learning. At the end of the lesson, pupils complete the remaining sections: one thing I have learned today and what I would like to find out more about. See the diagram for an example. This is also a good assessment for the learning plenary as it gives pupils the opportunity to really reflect on what they have learned in that lesson and it gives you ideas for future lessons.

It's also really important to give your pupils an overview of the whole unit of learning. If pupils are to be more independent and

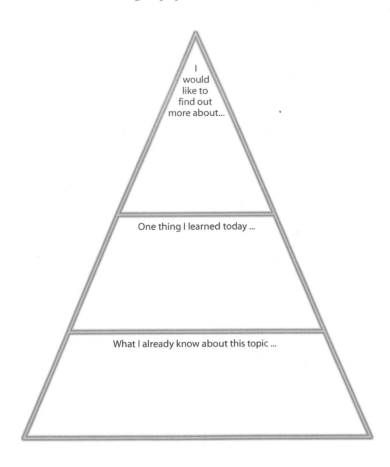

in control of their learning, then they need to know where they are going in that process. Pupils should have an understanding of the unit's contents, and the skills they can develop through that unit. In chapter 1.6 on personalizing learning, I included a template for an overview of the knowledge and skills that pupils can gain through a unit of work. This is an ideal tool for referring to at the start of each lesson. Better still, quiz all your class at the start of the lesson about what they learned in the previous lesson. You could adapt the learning pyramid so that its bottom level reads 'what I learned last lesson' instead. Ask pupils at random what they wrote down and allow class members to add more things to their pyramid as they hear from others in the room. This would get everyone in the class engaged and alert, and would help to contextualize the lesson's learning.

Unit or topic success criteria

It is always good to aim for something. So the series of lessons should have an overall aim that assesses how well pupils have performed and gives them, and you, clear criteria for success. This usually takes the form of an assignment or test. An assignment could be a piece of creative writing in which they have to employ key terms or concepts from the unit. Or it could be a report, a diagram, a flow chart, a PowerPoint presentation, a leaflet, and so on. It could be collaborative, such as a presentation or poster. A test could be a keywords test, a fill-in-the-blanks test or a more formal examination.

My two favourite summative assessments are to do with year 9 and ethics. The first one, after studying ethical stances and the events of the Holocaust, was to imagine that it was 1939 and they were in Germany. They knew what was about to happen, and had been asked by a friend who was a resistance fighter if they would help him to kill Hitler. They had to write a letter to their friend, using the key terms they had learned from the unit, explaining whether they would or would not help him. The other assignment I really enjoy marking is about virtues. Pupils learn about Aristotle's and Aquinas' virtue ethics, and learn about Benjamin Franklin's experiment to be more virtuous. Pupils replicate this experiment by picking one virtue and attempting to cultivate that virtue over one week. Their assessment is to write a report about how they got on trying to be extra generous/magnanimous/friendly/etc, often with hilarious results.

In all cases, pupils are aware of how they will be assessed and what we, as markers, are looking for. Later in this section, I have included a template for a unit overview sheet that you could share with pupils. It includes an explanation of the unit's main assessment activity and assessment objective criteria. My school continues to use and adapt National Curriculum levels, which I think work rather well. In Scotland, the old 5–14 levels – which served a similar purpose to the National Curriculum levels – have been replaced with the Experiences and Outcomes of the Curriculum for Excellence. These are also rather good, but I wonder if they'll need broken down into sub-levels (i.e. A/B/C) so you can monitor progress better across the year. Alternatively, you could simply create your own levels or grade boundaries depending on your department's practice.

Ideas to get you started

I've included a range of starters, middlers, and plenaries to get you started that can engage pupils with your lesson content, with you and with your subject in general. And I've included some advice about pupil presentations too. There are, however, a few things that you should always do in every lesson:

- Smile. Whatever mood you are really in doesn't matter: it is important to make sure you are in your creative state, so from the moment you see a pupil, smile! Act as though nothing is a problem for you and you are pleased to see them. It will make all the difference.

- Remember to say hello ('Good morning, class') – it's only polite – and say something nice about them ('It's good to see you again') to make them feel valued.

- Also remember that a pupil has only learned what they have memorized. If they don't remember it, they haven't learned it. If, during your lesson starter, you realize that the class in general has forgotten something, then look for ways to reintroduce the forgotten concept/information to reinforce it.

Lesson Starters: some thoughts

Imagine that you are about to start a lesson. When your pupils arrive in your classroom, you must, must, must remember that your pupils have a life outside of your classroom. This means that there is a period of time from the end of your last lesson and the start of this one during which pupils have experienced many other things. You certainly have, because contrary to popular pupil opinion, you don't live in your classroom. In fact, if you thought hard enough, you could probably list a hundred things you did since you saw your pupils last. And you have not been on the receiving end of lesson after lesson, homework after homework. So you need to bring pupils' minds to where they were in your last lesson: you need to revise what has been learned already.

Also, given that you haven't been responsible for their emotional welfare in that intervening time, you don't know what mood your pupils are going to be in. The teacher of their last lesson could have been your school's version of Grotbags, and they could all be really riled up and tense. Or they could be hyper because of the soft touch Joyce Grenfell-esque teacher who doesn't really have any classroom control. Or worse, some were with Grotbags while the others were with Joyce Grenfell, meaning you have a mixture of both tense and hyper.

Moreover, what about everything else going on? What about how well they are getting on with their friends? What about problems at home? What pressures and issues are affecting them? In many instances you just don't know; a lot may have happened since last lesson so pupils' behaviour, mood, attention and interest could be very different from the last time you saw them. It's worth remembering that your lesson is very unlikely to be the most important thing in their lives. You need to get their attention. A strict teacher will often do this with a shout and a bit of fear motivation. However, following the philosophy of the creative classroom means you need to bring them into the spirit and mindset of your lesson in a more positive fashion. So your lesson starters should be something of a motivational warm-up as well as a bit of revision.

Lesson Starters: some ideas

1. A moment's thought

Having welcomed your class, tell your pupils that you're going to give them a moment (thirty seconds to one minute, up to you) to recall everything they learned last lesson. They should jot down as many points as they can on a piece of paper or in the back of their exercise books.

- You might like to give them a minimum number of points to write down; three might be a good starting place.

- Make it into something of a game, pile on mock pressure as time runs out, give lots of motivational praise and/or encourage a little friendly rivalry with their neighbour to see how many points each has written down.

- If a pupil genuinely cannot remember anything from last lesson, then use a series of prompts with them as everyone else gets on with the activity. Ask them if they can remember the gist, or the topic. It may well be the case that they can remember some of it, but find it hard to write it down. This is ok. You might like to try the next idea instead if this is the case with many of your pupils.

- You could reward the person/people who got the most number of points, for example a credit for your school's merit system.

Without asking for hands up (it allows pupils to opt out too easily, particularly in this scenario), ask random pupils for one thing they wrote down on their list and, if the point is correct and relevant, ask the class how many got that on their list. Asking random pupils means that pupils make sure they are ready to answer and are therefore better engaged. Involving the whole class means that everyone gets involved and the pupil receives peer acknowledgement for getting it right. If the pupil is wrong, don't scold. Throw it open to the class to correct the misunderstanding, but do so in a friendly manner. For example, 'Thank you, but that's not everything we need to know, can anyone tell us what's missing?'

Incorporate this activity as part of your learning pyramid if you like and then make sure you make the link between what they've remembered and what they are about to learn in your lesson.

Just for fun, assuming that pupils wrote down their ideas on a piece of paper, get them to fold up the paper into paper aeroplanes. Place the waste bin in the middle of the room and get pupils to aim for the bin. There's no particular reason for this activity, other than to dispose of scrap paper in a reasonably kinaesthetic way. It will help your kinaesthetic pupils get involved in your lesson if they've had a chance to make something and move about a bit. If you are doing this with excitable pupils for the first time, explain to them that attempts to sabotage this game will result in points being deducted from your points system, or some other simple equivalent.

2.Think pair share

Follow the same steps as with *A moment's thought* but instead of a class discussion, get pupils to talk to their neighbour. Give pupils up to a minute to 'think' and then give pupils another minute to 'pair and share' what they've recalled with their neighbour. It's a less exposing way of achieving the same kind of revision as *A moment's thought*. Working in a pair will probably correct many mistakes, although if you're not sure, you can always still have the class feedback element too.

3. Bob if you ...

Bobbing is the art of raising yourself out of your seat a little bit, and then sitting back down. The effect is that you 'bob up' from your seat. It's the kinaesthetic equivalent of putting your hand up. Pupils find this a far more fun and interactive way of participating.

Simply question the class and get them to respond in the positive by bobbing up. So, for instance, you could say in History 'The Second World War began in 1939' and check for pupils' knowledge by seeing how many bobbed up in agreement. You could mix it in with false statements to see if you could catch anyone out. Alternatively you could use multiple-answer questions and get pupils to bob up for answer a, b, c or d.

4. Interactive fun

If you're lucky enough to have a projector or interactive whiteboard in your classroom, then you might like to use it to play warm-up games. For example, you could combine Bob if you... with Who Wants to be a Millionaire? which you can download from various websites. They tend to be customizable, so you can enter your own questions and answer options. Moreover they are free! You can also download other interactive games like Countdown and Blockbusters.

5. What am I?

Instead of asking a question, give them the answer and get them to work out what the question is. In Maths, you could give the answer '20' and pupils would have to think of all the ways to get to 20, and so on. In Geography you could start describing the features of something like an archipelago, and a pupil would have to guess what you are talking about. Or in Maths: 'I have four sides, one pair of parallel lines and no symmetry'. Answer: a trapezium.

6. Map it

When starting a new unit of work, get pupils to create the start of a map. Put the unit title in the centre, and the main ideas on branches. It's important that they make their own mind-maps so that they have a feeling of ownership over their work. Then at the start of each lesson, pupils add on details they have learned. For more information about how to map, see page 78.

7. Continuum

Pupils stand in line according to how they feel about a topic, discussion point, question and so forth. Those with positive feelings stand at one end of the line, those with neutral feelings in the middle, and those with negative feelings at the other end of the line. This can be used as the basis of a discussion between pupils with different opinions or as an indication about what pupils need to learn next.

8. Mnemonics

Get pupils to revise prior learning by making up a mnemonic in pairs to summarize and revisit what they've learned. You could ask pupils to volunteer the name of someone or something famous and then use that name or word to form the mnemonic. For instance, if they had picked Simon Cowell then they would need to collaborate with each other to make associations: S is for ...

9. Image Mnemonics

In Maths or the sciences, place a formula or equation on the whiteboard that they need to memorize from a previous lesson. For each part of the equation, pupils create an imaginative story by replacing each letter, number or symbol with an image that begins with that letter or represents that number or symbol. So, for example, $p \times r = g\text{-}32$ could become a **penguin timed** roger and hoped he would **equal** the gopher's score, but he was actually **32** seconds **faster** (for minus). The image of a penguin timing roger and the gopher is memorable and might help pupils to make the neural connections strong enough for the equation to stick in their minds. They won't always have to recall the image in the future, but they can if it helps, and the process of doing so will have helped them memorize it.

10. Open-ended questions

Put up a picture, object, quote, etc. on the whiteboard and ask pupils to respond to it. What do they think it might mean? What might it represent? If there are several images, which do they prefer and why? There shouldn't be any particular right or wrong response at this stage, just the opportunity for pupils to engage with something that represents the main aspect of the learning that will take place in the lesson.

11. Anagrams

Produce anagrams, or similar puzzles, of key words – either ones to be learned in the lesson or from previous lessons that are relevant in this lesson. The anagrams could be devised by the teacher or by groups or partners in the class to test each other. You could even take the register while they got on with them.

12. Bingo

Put up a list of 16 key words or concepts from the unit so far. Either get pupils to make their own 4 × 4 grids in the back of their exercise books, or hand out a blank template to them. Pupils should jot down the 16 words and concepts in random order in their grid. Some teachers prefer to make up several versions of the grid, complete with all the key terms, for the pupils in advance. I prefer for pupils to produce their own so that everyone's is unique. Once everyone is ready, pick a key term and come up with a cryptic definition of it. Pupils have to recognize the key term from your description and circle it. If they don't recognize it, they miss out. Whoever gets four in a row first (horizontal, diagonal or vertical) should shout out Bingo!

13. Who am I?

Write key terms on a series of post-it notes. Stick a post-it note to each pupil's head and get them to ask their partners questions about who/what they are. Their partners can only respond 'yes' or 'no'. A much more fun and kinaesthetic version of what am I?

14. You Say We Pay

In pairs, one pupil faces towards the interactive whiteboard and the other pupil faces away. Put pictures up of things that have been learned recently, or things that are relevant to the lesson, and the pupil facing the whiteboard has to describe the image without saying exactly what it is. The other pupil has to guess it. You can make this extra fun by listing words that are 'taboo' and cannot be said as part of the pupil's attempt to describe the image to their partner.

15. Pictionary

Divide pupils in to two groups. Give everyone in group one a list of key terms that they have to convey to a partner in group two. The only way they are allowed to inform their partner of this key term is by drawing a sketch of it, like in the board game. They cannot say anything, or gesture anything; they can only draw. There are various ways to do this. If your classroom is arranged in rows then everyone in rows one and three are in group one, and everyone in rows two and four are in group two. That way pupils in group one only need to turn to the row behind them to find a partner. Alternatively, you could make this a whole class activity by dividing the class in to two or more competing groups. Invite one person at a time from each group to come up to draw a key term (that you give them) for members of their group to guess – one point for every correct guess.

Lesson Middlers: some thoughts

Ok, so 'middlers' is not a word. But I'm sure you understand what I mean. Middlers are the main activities of your lesson. By necessity they may well involve large amounts of written work – for instance, GCSE coursework or an essay – but remember that pupils do not learn only if they can present you with neatly written answers to textbook questions. Remember that they are more likely to learn better, and recall the information, through more active methods and can then produce superior written work as a summative exercise.

One of the things you will notice is that the activities often involve providing pupils with the core information and getting them to be creative with it. Remember, this is the point of creative teaching – yes, you need to feel and be creative, come up with ideas and engage them through your personality and through your chosen activities, but, moreover, you want to facilitate an active creative approach among your pupils. So it is important not to spoon-feed them; you are aiming to give them independence and responsibility.

Lesson Middlers: Some ideas

1. The learning factor

This is a really simple and very flexible idea where pupils can work individually, in pairs or in groups. Simply give out the information you want pupils to learn, it could be pages from a textbook, newspaper articles, a video or something else. Give them a time limit, maybe 20 minutes, to come up with a song or a rap to perform to the rest of the class about the given topic. You can stipulate certain things they must include, but I am sure you'll be impressed with just how much they include themselves.

2. Drawing blind

If you have an image of something pupils need to be familiar with, such as a place of worship, a geographical feature or location, parts of an experiment, or maybe the mechanism of an object, then get pupils to copy it down from the interactive whiteboard. However, the pupil drawing it should have their back to the image and should be relying on their partner to describe the image for them, attempting to communicate well enough to get a close replica of the image! It is great fun, and excellent for all sorts of communication and interpersonal skills. Pupils should then label the image with relevant information and amend any serious errors!

3. Conversion

Pupils simply need to convert the given information into some other form. It could be into 'txt spk', or into a flow diagram, a map, a table, a picture, or even a play!

4. Creative Discussion

Pair up pupils and give them a question or issue to discuss for two minutes. They should spend time listening to each other's opinions and, for higher ability or older pupils, they should then see where they have similarities and differences of opinions. Everyone then gets up and swaps partners. This can be done in a variety of ways. You could be very orderly and have arranged pupils to sit in two circles – an inner and an outer circle – facing each other. This has the advantage of being able quickly to move pupils in one circle round a bit so they find new partners. The disadvantage is that you will need to have moved the furniture in your room, which is part of creative teaching.

However, in the event of furniture moving not being possible, you could arrange new pairings in different ways. You could tell pupils to find a new partner who 'is sitting furthest from you', 'is a member of the same sex', or the other sex, 'has the same coloured hair', 'whose name shares a letter with a letter with yours', and so on. The new partnership has to explain their previous partner's point of view and then take the discussion on further. It's great for listening skills, which should wake your pupils up! Plus it is an inventive way to spice up discussions.

5. Advertising

You always remember the things you see in adverts, so why not use adverts as a teaching tool? This activity takes two forms. Again, provide pupils with the information, but this time get them to prepare a billboard advertisement as if the information were a film or a product to be sold. Alternatively, get your pupils to write and perform a movie trailer of the information. I really enjoyed my Year 12's movie trailer for 'Aristotle: the greatest philosopher that walked this Earth'!

6. The little things

Sometimes it is the simplest ideas that work the best. If you can use chocolates or sweets, then you are on to a winner. Demonstrate the causes of erosion by getting the class to put a sweet in their mouths. Demonstrate the Ontological Argument for the existence of God by using chocolate – which is better, chocolate that you imagine or chocolate that is real? You can be healthy and use fruit if you prefer. Anything that helps pupils visualize what you are talking about is helpful. You could demonstrate the effects of rationing by putting on your table a day's worth of food allowance, but it would be far simpler to pour out some jelly beans on a desk, tell them the beans represent how much they get to eat daily today and then separate off roughly the right proportion to represent how much they would have got after the Second World War.

7. Mastermind

Pick four students in the class to become contestants in a special game of Mastermind. Splitting the class into four groups, each group has the responsibility of prepping their contestants in their specialist subject: the topic they have just finished studying. Having given an appropriate amount of time to prepare their contestant – I suggest a maximum of 15 minutes to make it fun and intensive – send the contestants outside the room to wait to be called to The Chair (or teacher's chair). You'll need to have prepared some questions to ask the contestants before the lesson: I suggest around 15 to 20 questions. Ask each contestant the same questions and watch while the rest of the class squirm knowing the answers! In that lesson, students would have taught their peers everything from your course, and then heard it repeated four times. Contestants, too, will have made a concerted effort to memorize the lesson or topic content. All lots of fun.

8. The Marketplace

This is a favourite of mine, and it is good for introducing concepts, delving deeper into one or more concepts or revising the concepts. Put students into groups of around four and allocate to each group a key aspect of the topic that they will have to teach to other pupils in the room. For instance, in a GCSE topic each group could represent one aspect listed on the unit's specification. Give them some resources to help, and also some large paper and pens. Tell each group to come up with a 'market stall' that 'sells' that concept to everyone else. This could be in the form of a task that visitors to their market stall would have to complete – a crossword puzzle, anagram, a set of cryptic questions, and so forth. Or it could be to share a memory trick like a mnemonic, or a diagram, a picture that represents it, and so on – especially if this is a revision session. This activity works best when you've given a clear structure to the lesson, so put up timings on the board. Obviously this will vary depending on the content they are working with and the length of your school's lessons. But as a rough guide I suggest:

- Research Stage: 20 minutes.
  During this time, the group must work together to find out the necessary information and produce their poster/ activity ready to teach other pupils. If producing a poster, I suggest that you limit the number of words they can use on the poster – maybe to about ten words. This encourages them to be more creative and interact better with their peers when teaching them.

- Peer Teaching Stage: 10 minutes.
  When the research stage is finished, one pupil becomes the 'stallholder'. It is their job to stay at the market stall and convey the information to the others in the class. It is best if they stand to do this, and better still try to create a marketplace atmosphere by calling out things like 'two facts for a pound', 'come and buy some lovely information' and so on. All of the other members of the group should visit the other market stalls that have information on the different topics you've selected. It usually works best if they have a template to write down the information from around the room. I've included the sort of thing I'm talking about below. Your strategic pupils will have divvied up between them who will visit each group so they do not miss out any of the market stalls.

Group topic	Fact 1	Fact 2	Fact 3	Fact 4
1				
2				
3				
4				
5				

- Group Sharing Stage: 5 minutes.
  Having gone round the room successfully, the rest of the group report back to their stallholder and help him or her, and everyone else in the group, fill in a summary sheet too.

- Quiz Stage: 10 minutes.
  To assess their knowledge you could then have a quiz where each team is competing with the others. There's lots of ways of doing this, adapting any of the material from the starter, middler or plenary part of this chapter. You might decide, for example, that should the stallholder be able to answer a question without having to confer with the other group members then their group will receive more points than if a group member has to help.

9. Verbal football

Go through materials and either you or the pupils devise some questions, or maybe they can come from a textbook. Split the class in half and have them sit facing each other. Ask one half a question, and if someone from that team is able to get it right then the (metaphorical) ball stays in play with that team. Otherwise the other half get asked the next question. When one half gets three questions in a row right they score a goal. The team with the most goals wins. But everyone should find that they now remember more of that topic.

10. Trench warfare

An unusual twist on verbal football. Split your class into two halves. Give each pupil at least three sheets of paper. On each sheet, each pupil must write one question about the topic they are studying and the answer that goes with that question. Appoint one person to be commander of their 'squadron'; the commander should make sure that there are no repeated questions and organize the questions into easy, medium and hard difficulty. Clear the classroom of desks and chairs. Using some of the desks and chairs, get pupils to create a 'trench' or barricade that their team can hide behind. Having decided which squadron can start first, allow the commander to pick who can 'fire' an easy/medium/hard question at the other squadron first. If someone from the other squadron calls out the wrong answer then the questioner should turn their sheet of paper into ammunition (quickly scrunch it up or turn it into a paper plane or something) and should try to throw it at the person who got it wrong. If the other squadron gets it right, throw the ammunition at them anyway! If a squadron gives the right answer, it is their turn to 'fire' a question. If a squadron gets it wrong, then the other squadron is able to 'fire' another question. You should keep score of the number of correct answers on both sides. Needless to say this is a messy and daft activity, but a lot of fun with the right class. You really need to be sure that you've got a lot of reciprocal trust with this group – who should probably be older rather than younger.

11. Press Conference

Having spent a few lessons on a new topic, tell the class that they are going to be journalists and that you have invited an expert to answer their questions. If you can, set up a podium in your classroom and a sign that says 'press conference'. Give them a few minutes to come up with some questions. You might need to give them some resources to work from, or you might not: up to you. Set a time limit for the press conference, say 10 or 15 minutes, and tell pupils that they need to raise their hand if they want to ask their question – just like journalists do at a real press conference. The expert is either you, an older pupil who might know the material really well, or a colleague. Award small prizes to questioners, if you wish. Encourage pupils to take notes; you might like to follow this activity up with a news report – either a written one, or a role-play of a TV news report (see below).

12. Not the nine o'clock news

This activity can either follow on from the activity above, or stand alone. Put pupils into groups of four or five. Tell them that they have to create a news bulletin about a given topic. Either give the whole class the same topic, or give each group something different to do. Give them around twenty minutes to prepare (less if this is following on from the press conference), complete with on-the-scene reporters and expert commentators in the newsroom. Groups should then perform their news bulletin to the rest of the class. If each group is reporting on something different, then you'll need to encourage the rest of the class to take notes on what they see. You might feel the need to produce a sheet for each group that lists essential facts they must communicate in their report, and then give a version to the rest of the class with blanks that need to be filled in.

13. Daytime TV

Similar to the news activity above, but this time pupils recreate a daytime magazine TV programme. Arrange for pupils to become the presenters (one male, one female) and one or more guests to interview. You might like to prepare question cards for the presenters, or you might like to let them ask their own questions. The rest of the class play the role of the audience at home. They should all write a question they would like to ask the guests as part of a 'phone in'. They can write these questions down on post-its and then hand them to you, and you decide which questions will get asked. These questions can then be read out from the back of the room and answered by the guests as if they had come over the phone.

14. Human Diagrams

Get pupils to reproduce something like a bar graph or line graph by using their bodies. Either you or different groups can direct the class accordingly. I did this once when teaching music and it was lots of fun. I got year 7 pupils to come up with tunes in their groups and they had to become human musical notes. I created musical staves on the floor using masking tape and they had to lie down and form the right sort of musical notes in the right places. It was lots of fun, an excellent kinaesthetic activity and it really helped to bring music notation to life – quite literally! You'll need lots of space and you might want to use a digital camera to take photos so you can refer back to the activity in future lessons. Another variation of this is to give pupils roles to play in a system or process and then get them to act the whole process out. This can be useful for teaching students about the human body, computer concepts, geographical terms and so on.

15. Compare and Contrast

This activity can really help your pupils iron out any areas of potential confusion or lack of clarity. Organize pupils into pairs or small groups, get them to make a grid like the one below on a flip chart or on A3 paper. They work in groups to make a bullet-pointed list of important similarities and differences between the two concepts. Either they work from their existing notes, or from new resources you give them. This could be used in any subject to help teach almost any pair of similar concepts. For example: fractions and percentages, osmosis and diffusion, shares and bonds, commas and semicolons and so on.

	Similarities	
Comparing [x] and [y]	They both:	
	Differences	
	x... but y...	y... but x ...

Lesson Enders: some thoughts

It is important to end the lesson neatly and clearly. It is best if you can recap what has been learned in the lesson by testing them quickly; this is an opportunity to incorporate some assessment for learning and for personalized learning – to get pupils to reflect on how they themselves have progressed.

And as 80 per cent of detail can be forgotten within 24 hours of learning it, it makes a big difference if you reinforce it before they go. While pupils will inevitably forget information and details you teach them if they do not reinforce it in their own time (the neural pathways will degrade over time if they are not lit up often enough), if you reinforce the learning before you dismiss your class then that 80 per cent becomes more like 40 per cent or 50 per cent.

If you also recap and test their memories at the start of your next lesson with them, then again you significantly reduce the amount they will forget because you are lighting up the right neural pathways. Many of the plenary ideas below can also be used as lesson starters, or even as lesson middlers, so please be flexible with these ideas and make them your own.

Lesson Enders: some ideas

1. Quick-fire list

Get pupils to jot down five things they have learned in your lesson. If there's time, get them to explain one or two of these things to a neighbour.

2. On trial

Get the pupils to vote, as if they were a jury, on the most important thing or things learned in your lesson. This does a great job of highlighting the main ideas.

3. Mission completed?

State the lesson objective again – can your pupils fulfil the objective? Ask random pupils (do not accept hands-up as it allows other pupils to become passive). You could get them to think, pair, share first.

4. Newsflash

Pupils simply prepare a quick news report on your lesson. Get them to perform it if there's time – you can always pair up the groups so that they can perform to each other instead of the whole class. Better still, get them to perform it at the start of next lesson as a recap activity.

5. Tableau

Get pupils to form a tableau – a sort of 'freeze-frame moment' – of something learned in the lesson (for example, a scene in a book they are reading, or a nature cycle represented in human form) and then quiz individuals in the tableau about the 'character' they are playing.

6. Txt the teacher

Hand each pupil a post-it note. Tell them to 'send' you a text message version of what they have learned from the lesson, or something similar that matches your lesson's success criteria. Having written their text message, they should stick the post-it notes up somewhere prominent so you and the rest of the class can read them all.

7. In so many words

Ask a random pupil for a number between five and ten. Then tell pupils to individually write up with a sentence with the amount of words that was volunteered. It could be to sum up what they learned today. Or perhaps you'd like a list of key terms or ideas learned in the lesson instead. So if your random pupil says seven, you say 'Okay, write a seven word sentence about what you learned today' or 'Okay, list seven things you learned today'. You could ask for a number between ten and twenty if you really want to set a challenge.

8. Charades

Invite one or more pupils to the front of the room to perform a mime that represents something that they learned today. The rest of the class have to guess what it is.

9. Headlines

In pairs, pupils come up with a newspaper headline that sums up what they've learned in the lesson. Tell them to focus on what the key issue is, and how to get people's attention on to it. Get them to call out their newspaper headlines as if they are selling newspapers ('Read all about it, Oxbow lakes in meandering crisis!'). Better still, hand out A3 paper for them to write their headlines in large letters so they can hold them up when they become newspaper sellers.

10. Hangman

Pick a key term they should know from the lesson and play hangman with the class. Alternatively they could play hangman in groups, with each person in the group taking it in turns to come up with a word.

11. Advertising Slogans

Similar to the headlines plenary, challenge pupils in pairs to come up with an advertising slogan to sell the lesson's main idea. For example, a lesson on the calculation of Average Rate of Return on an investment could be given the slogan "things that make you go ARR". Things like this really help pupils to remember the main points, and even some details, for future lessons.

12. The Final Word

Get all pupils ready to leave, packed up and standing behind their chairs. Each pupil has to state one key word/term/idea they have learned in the lesson (or in the topic) before they can leave, without repeating what someone else has already said. If they repeat something already said, they can't leave until two more pupils have had their turn and they can come up with another unique key term. A quicker version of this plenary is to pick at random one person from each table or row to give a key term in order to dismiss the whole table or row.

13. Call my bluff

In groups of three, give pupils a key word. They have to come up with the correct definition and two false definitions. In their group, each pupil takes it in turns to share a definition with another group. The other group has to identify which definition is correct. Alternatively you could do this as a whole class or by creating teams of three or four groups, with each group identifying which definition they think is correct.

14. Match Report

Go all John Motson with your pupils. Give them a reminder about things they have learned in the last few lessons and get them to individually write a 'match report' that describes everything that went on. It doesn't just have to include the lesson content, it could also include who scored the goals (i.e. which pupils contributed what) and decisions by the ref or the team's manager (i.e. you!). Select pupils at random to read theirs out.

15. Beat the teacher

Not literally. You give a summary of what they have learned so far (either verbally or on the board) that contains some mistakes. Tell pupils how many mistakes there are and they have to spot them. To make sure that everyone participates, think pair share it.

FACT BOX – PUPIL PRESENTATIONS

It is really commonplace, and creative, to get groups of pupils to prepare and give a presentation to the rest of the class – normally on a topic that only they have researched. From an independent learning perspective, this sort of activity is brilliant. But there are a number of pitfalls. The three main ones are the passive group member(s) who don't really do anything throughout the whole process and negatively affect the group dynamic; what the rest of the class does during the presentation in order to participate; how the group is assessed for their presentation.

Group dynamics:

The best and simplest thing to do here is to give everyone a clear role to play. According to Jenny Rice from De Montfort University, the following roles are very effective at getting everyone in the group to work:

- group leader/facilitator, to co-ordinate strategy and plan ahead

- timekeeper, to hold everyone to deadlines

- task monitor, to check progress and nudge things along

- finisher, to tie up the ends

Everyone should be a researcher, and if they are using PowerPoint then everyone should make at least one slide and put their initials in the bottom corner. Other roles you could add if required are: a quality checker (to make sure everything is up to scratch) and a resource manager (to look after pens, paper, computer files, etc.). If someone doesn't do their part it is far easier to identify them this way, and it gives you and the rest of the group something tangible and quantifiable to put to the under-performing pupil.

Class participation:

When you set the presentation task, make it very clear to each group what you expect from their presentation. This should be in the form of three or four main points that they must cover. Create a handout for the rest of the pupils to fill in during each group's presentation that simply asks them to note down details under each main point. This way, the rest of the class have a record of what the presentation was about. I've included a handout template for you below.

Group Name	Presentation Topic
Main Point	Details from presentation
1. *[teacher inserts information here]*	*[pupils insert information here during and just after presentation]*
2.	

3.	
4.	

Assessment:

I suggest that you appoint a couple of judges from the class to judge the presentations and give feedback. Feedback should principally be about presentation skills and should be more positive than negative, 'Things we thought went well were ...'. Anything negative should be framed as constructive, the best way to put this is: 'it would have been even better if ...'. I suggest the following criteria that the judges could use to give their feedback:

- eye contact
- body language
- clarity of speaking
- structure
- resources
- group participation
- whether they covered the main points adequately
- and the creativity of the presentation

The judges could also give a score out of four for overall presentation and overall content. You should also give your feedback along with the judges, but the power and appreciation of peer feedback cannot be underestimated here.

Group work with an ensuing presentation to the class is an excellent creative and independent learning model to use, and if you apply the strategies above you should find that your pupils will get so much more out of the activity than they might otherwise.

Excellent planning

Right, so you've got this far in the book. Well done. You've read up on all the things a creative teacher should know about. You've done the audits and tasks thus far, and now you've got some ideas from the last section, and you are raring to go. My first piece of advice is to just try some of the activities out. Pick one that seems to fit a lesson you've got coming up and just do it. See how it goes. See how it feels.

Assuming that went well, then continue to sprinkle what you currently do with some new ideas from this book and let things take shape gradually.

But if you really want to take the bull by its horns, then excellent and thorough planning is the key to bringing all this together and making successful, creative lessons the norm. There are three levels to this: the topic or unit as a whole, the lesson itself and what you communicate to pupils.

FACT BOX – TOP TEN THINGS TO HAVE IN YOUR MIND WHEN PLANNING

1 **The pupils themselves** – what particular pupils do you need to consider? What are their character strengths? Remember that they have done and learned lots of things since seeing you last

2 **Rapport** – how does this lesson improve your rapport with the class? How will you make sure they feel secure and valued?

3 **Structure** – how will you make sure that the lesson content is clearly delivered, expectations are clear and pupils remain on task, focussed and well behaved?

4 **Creativity** – which creative techniques could you use? How does this lesson engage their RAS? What's in it for them?

---

5 **Success Criteria** – it is really important to have clear objectives that you share with your class at the start of every lesson; this way both you and they know where the lesson is going, and if they have successfully met your expectations.

6 **Independent Learning** – how is this lesson pupil-centred and not teacher-centred? How does this lesson encourage a growth mindset?

7 **Personalized Learning** – in what ways are pupils encouraged to be aware of, and reflect upon, how the lesson helps to develop the skills they identified in their target setting?

8 **Assessment for Learning** – how will you get feedback about pupils' progress and how will they assess their understanding and progress?

9 **Learning to learn/study skills** – how does this lesson help them memorize the information? How do you ensure a mix of right and left brain activities (VAK, multiple intelligences, etc.)?

10 **Your creative state** – how creative do you feel today? How is your emotional intelligence? Are there stresses or other things lowering your mood? How can you feel more relaxed and focussed?

The topic or unit as a whole

I've created a table below for planning your scheme of work. It follows on from the creative audit you did at the end of section one. You can download an editable version from this book's companion website.

	Unit Title:	Knowledge pupils must learn:				Skills pupils could gain:					
Lesson Number and Title	Knowledge to gain	Skills to gain	Lesson success criteria	Creative Starter – include the reasons for using this starter	Creative Middlers – include the reasons for using these activities	Creative Ender – include the reason for using this plenary	Assessment for Learning opportunities	Personalized Learning opportunities	Independent Learning opportunities	Study Skills employed to improve memory (including VAK & MI)	Resources needed
1.											
2.											
3.											
4.											
5.											

The Lesson Itself

There's obviously a variety of ways to plan a lesson, so may be you'll be happy using your own methods. But if you'd like a template to work from, especially to get started, then here's one to try. Again, this is downloadable from the companion website.

Lesson Title: Topic: _____ (lesson ___ of _____) Year group: Class:		
Success Criteria to share with pupils	Main Lesson Activities	Lesson Plenary
Lesson Starter		Review of lesson Rapport:
Notes re structure, discipline, rapport and support	Opportunities Independent Learning:	Structure: Creativity:
Resources required	Personalized Learning: Study Skills: Assessment for Learning: Use of (highlight the following that apply): left/right brain Visual Auditory Kinaesthetic MI: linguistic; logic; musical; kinaesthetic; spatial; interpersonal; intrapersonal; naturalist	Independent Learning: Personalized Learning: Study Skills: Assessment for Learning: Your creative state: Overall pupil response:

What you communicate to pupils

I suggest that at the start of every unit, you use the following template to make a handout to pupils about the unit. It can be used throughout the unit to help with assessment for learning and as a reference point for connecting the learning from one lesson to the next. It follows on from some of the material earlier in the book. An editable version is downloadable from the companion website.

<u>Pupil Unit Overview Sheet</u>

Unit Title: [enter title here]

Key Concepts:

1 *(place picture or text here)*	2	3	4	5

Unit Overview

	Lesson Title (or series of lessons title)
1	
2	
3	

4	
5	
6	
7	

By the end of this unit you should have developed:

Knowledge	Skills
1.	1.
2.	2.
3.	3.
4.	4.
5.	5.
6.	6.
7.	7.

Main Assessment Activity:

{explain here}

Assessment Criteria

AO1: *state what this assessment outcome is (e.g. describe and explain …)*

Level 8	Level 7	Level 6	Level 5
Enter criteria here			

AO2: *state what this assessment outcome is (e.g. evaluate and reason …)*

Level 8	Level 7	Level 6	Level 5
Enter criteria here			

[add further AOs if required]

Assessment for Learning – to be filled out at the start of the unit

The lesson or knowledge I am most interested in is:

The skill I would most like to develop is:

Assessment for Learning – to be filled out at the end of the unit

What I think I did well ...	Even better if ...
Teacher's targets for me	My targets for the next unit

Chapter 3
The Creative School

In this section:

3.1 Schools That Are Getting it Right

The team of presenters at Learning Performance have, between them, conducted over 8,000 workshops in schools, meeting well over one million pupils. These are some of their best memories of schools and the teaching staff who have engaged pupils successfully in the creative learning process ...

'There was this one school I visited which had a really different feel to it. There was a kind of buzz in the air and it was a very cheerful, friendly place. But that isn't what made it different. Plenty of schools are like that. What was noticeable was that age wasn't much of a barrier. In fact

pupils walked around in mixed age groups. You see, they had what the school called 'vertical forms' – instead of grouping their form classes by year group they organized them in house teams where Year 7 through to Year 11 pupils were together in the same form class. The school swears by this system. They told me it created scope for mentoring younger pupils, and indeed it encouraged greater maturity among their younger pupils as they were in direct contact with their older peers. It goes to show you what a little out-of-the-box thinking can do.'

'I've been visiting the same school each year for the last six years. When I first arrived the teachers were understandably sceptical about what I was teaching their pupils, but by the end of the day they were on board and seemed really enthused by the ideas we were talking about. The next time I went back, one of the teachers greeted me with a big smile and took me to her classroom to show me what she had been up to since the last time I was there. She had got her pupils mapping out their work, and there must have been a hundred association maps around the room, all produced by her pupils. She told me that they used to do brainstorms, but since I demonstrated how to map things out she'd gone map crazy. She told me that pupils loved doing them as they were colourful and almost therapeutic to do, but they were great for summarizing and reinforcing all the information they had been learning. She says she gets less of a 'brain drain' when she tests pupils or revisits topics that they have mapped out. I find that the more creative schools are the ones where teachers are keen to show me what they do in their classrooms, like this lady was.'

'I was doing an INSET day in a school, talking about the need to appeal to pupils' left and right brains. One of the maths teachers came up to me during the break and told me about his absolutely brilliant idea: darts. He got his pupils to play darts

(I assume the Velcro variety, but you never know, it might be the real thing). They played darts and had to add up the score as quickly as possible and subtract it from the overall score. The pupils got competitive – in a good way – as they all tried to call out the correct score before anyone else did. They all had fun, and they were all doing mental arithmetic. Who'd have thought it possible?!'

'One very telling thing about schools is how willing staff are to join in with our activities. If they just sit in the corner marking work or, worse still, reading the paper, then you know that this is a school that is missing a trick. I know that staff have pressures to get work done, and marking is very important, but sometimes you can just tell that that member of staff is just disillusioned with their job. In schools that are more enjoyable places for both staff and pupils you'll find that the teachers will join in. They might just help pupils with the activities as we do them. Or they might be willing to come up to the front with me and demonstrate something. I have a very fond memory of a head teacher who helped me teach the pupils the kinaesthetic way to learn Japanese numbers, you know 'Itchy, knee, sun ...'. He knew it and had a whale of a time getting the pupils to do it. They responded well and clearly liked him. It makes so much of a difference if this kind of creative input comes from the top.'

'One school I visited had focused on languages and, as a way to engage pupils, one of the language teachers had translated scripts of tv shows and got the pupils to perform them. Pupils didn't necessarily know all the language, but they learned it pretty quickly because they all recognized the episode and so were able to relate directly to what was being said. In lots of schools I go to, pupils rate language subjects as some of their least favourite usually because they don't see it as relevant. But not at this school, the kids loved it.'

'Manners make a big difference. In some schools, and it can be anywhere in the country, pupils don't have manners. They don't seem to respect the school or the people in it and, as a result, don't seem to care very much about learning. But in schools where the pupils are nice to you and to each other they are more ready to learn. I went to one school and just as I got out of my car a pupil asked me if I wanted a sweet and I just knew I was going to have a good day! This was reflected across the whole school as far as I could see. There was no animosity in my group, everyone was friendly, everyone seemed to enjoy themselves and had a great time learning. You couldn't achieve that sort of situation in a school where pupils didn't have manners. A friendly environment is essential I think.'

3.2 The Philosophy of the Creative School

There are a lot of competing philosophies out there for schools to adopt. Many of them amount to the same sort of thing. So I'm not going to promote a one-size-fits-all policy here.

I am assuming that if you are reading this section, you are either in a leadership position in the school, or are part of a learning and teaching focus group in your school, and you like the sorts of things you've read so far in this book, including the examples of schools that are 'getting it right' above. If you are not in a leadership or focus group role, but feel that your school needs a more cohesive approach to its learning and teaching ethos then please read on too and see if you feel inspired to activate something creative in your school.

A school that feels that it wants to improve its learning and teaching – which has to involve making it more creative – will need a coherent framework and an accessible vocabulary for doing so that is clearly and fully supported from the top. It doesn't have to be that the head teacher leads on this, but the head teacher and the leadership team must be seen to be driving change forward.

Models and Buy-in

There are some good models out there. I rather like the former QCA's Personal, Learning and Thinking Skills model (PLTS). It simply identifies six skills that, along with English, Maths and ICT, are essential to developing life skills. These are the capacity to be:

- Independent Enquirers
- Creative Thinkers
- Reflective Learners
- Team Workers
- Self-managers
- Effective Participators

The new Curriculum for Excellence in Scotland is centred around four very similar skills called the Four Capacities (listed below). The CfE is a progressive skills-based, inter-disciplinary curriculum which is extremely impressive and might be of interest to newly formed academies in the rest of the UK looking for some inspiration. What I like about it is that every aspect of a pupil's experience of school, their experiences and outcomes, to use the CfE vocabulary, is underpinned by the skills sets outlined by the Four Capacities which are designed to help young people become:

1. Responsible Citizens
2. Successful Learners

3. Effective Contributors

4. Confident Individuals

The Campaign for Learning propagates 5Rs for effective lifelong learning:

1. Readiness

2. Resourcefulness

3. Resilience

4. Responsibility

5. Reflectiveness

All of these are good. Guy Claxton's *Building Learning Power* (2002) and his associated company, *The Learning Organisation*, also produce a range of materials that support these areas. He has also devised his own framework and vocabulary, again designed to sit atop a range of learning and teaching initiatives.

But the problem with any framework, any vocabulary, is buy-in. Buy-in from teachers, pupils, parents and, of course, governors. When I first started at my school in 2007, the then head teacher announced at the teachers' INSET at the start of the year that he was slashing the amount of homework we were allowed to set by 75 per cent and that all pupils would be encouraged to do their own independent study. He did this without consultation with anyone, and without a really clear framework for implementing the change. As you can imagine there was uproar and confusion among the staff. And while the idea became very popular with the pupils when they realized that they didn't have so much directed time at home, it was very unpopular with the parents, as their children suddenly had nothing academic to occupy them in the evenings and weekends, and soon the complaints came in.

I was approached, given my role with Learning Performance, to rescue independent study and formulate a clear plan for its integration into the school's fabric. I developed a routine that pupils should follow with their independent study, which was principally a regular revision slot at home, and set up means to monitor pupils' progress at school. I held a parents' information evening, pupil workshops and assemblies, produced resources and led some staff CPD. That communication and structure was vital in getting the buy-in that was so very much needed. Everyone was pleased with the outcome, and it even made the national news. Evidently, the building blocks of rapport, structure and creativity that I used earlier in this book, still applies at a whole-school level.

I would also suggest that the best way to sum up and establish your creative school's philosophy is in a vision statement. If we use Tuckman's forming/storming/norming/performing model of group development (1965), you'll need to start by forming a team of staff who are interested in promoting a more creative outlook for the school. They should obviously be a mix of personalities and represent all areas of the curriculum. They need to storm a list of values that you and they want to see employed at every level of pupils' experience in the school; this should also be done in conjunction with pupils and, ideally, parents and governors too. From there, a vocabulary can be established to be shared by departments and pupils to express those values. And, from there, you can establish a vision statement that sits atop of the values and vocabulary that aids a norming of creative practices from both pupils and staff, and then reach the performing level – where everything is essentially a smooth operation.

Values and vocabulary

In the last section I provided a 'top ten' list of things to consider when planning creative lessons. I would suggest that this list is also applicable if you are considering a whole-school model. I will go through each one in turn, asking questions to help you reflect on your school's current performance in each area, and advice on what you might like to look for in the future.

The pupils themselves. How well do school leaders know the pupils in the school? Can you claim that every pupil is known by at least one member of staff? How quickly and efficiently are special educational needs identified and communicated to staff, parents and relevant bodies? What provision have you got in place to handle emotional issues and how adequate are they? How well is pupil voice represented and to what extent does it help pupils feel that they are involved with the ethos and safe running of pupil life in the school? How proud are pupils of their school? To what degree are pupils happy, safe and achieving their potential?

That last question relates to a Scottish audit that I highly recommend to everyone else. It comes from the GIRFEC model (getting it right for every child) which aims to ensure comprehensive pastoral care. I suggest you look it up on the Scottish government's website. It outlines eight areas of care that aim to ensure that pupils feel they can grow and develop to be:

- **Healthy**, experiencing the highest standards of physical and mental health, and supported to make healthy safe choices

- **Achieving**, receiving support and guidance in your learning – boosting skills, confidence and self-esteem

- **Nurtured**, having a nurturing and stimulating place to live and grow

- **Active**, offered opportunities to take part in a wide range of activities – helping them to build a fulfilling and happy future

- **Respected**, to be given a voice and involved in the decisions that affect their wellbeing

- **Responsible**, taking an active role within school and communities

- **Included**, receiving help and guidance to overcome social, educational, physical and economic inequalities; accepted as a full member of the communities in which they live and learn

- **Safe**, protected from abuse, neglect or harm

I created a wellbeing questionnaire for my sixth formers based on this model, and you can download a copy of it from the companion website.

Further to this, there is an extraordinarily impressive movement towards wellbeing in schools at present. If we are saying that pupils need to feel safe, valued and happy in order to develop lifelong independent learning skills, then we need to encourage that independence and responsibility when it comes to their wellbeing as well as their learning. Ian Morris' Learning to Ride Elephants: Teaching Wellbeing and Happiness in Schools, also published by Continuum, is excellent and I cannot endorse it enough. Ian worked at Wellington College, where he essentially rewrote the PSHE curriculum to be less catastrophic and more in tune with real personal development through positive psychology, resilience, mindfulness, ancient wisdom and a healthy dose of common sense. One of my current responsibilities in the school I work in is to co-ordinate PSHE, and I have recently embarked on a mission to reform our current lessons to incorporate much of what is in his book.

I think my overall point here is that pupils need to feel valued and included in the life of the school. In order to achieve this, their basic needs must be met so that they feel safe and secure – while there is little schools can do about a pupil's home environment, a school should feel like a safe haven to a student. This should lead to an affinity for the school and an affection for all it stands for. So the vision statement needs to be highly accessible to them, not something they deride regularly (although there will always be a few who will) or seen as irrelevant to their experience of school. In order to make the values and vision come alive, I would advise getting your pupil council, or a pupil panel, to contribute to the process of forming a vision statement and set of values. This could be done through an activity such as an appreciative enquiry.

> *Examples of relevant values and vocabulary that could become mainstream in a creative school: wellbeing, affinity, pride, respect, nurtured, resilience, included, valued, happy, safe.*

FACT BOX – APPRECIATIVE ENQUIRY

At the core of Appreciative Enquiry is the idea that what people focus on becomes their reality. That is to say, focus on the positive and there will be a more positive future; focus on the negative and there will be a more negative future. So don't look at what is wrong with the school, that would be too easy, focus on what's right about it instead.

The AE model has four stages: discover, dream, design and deliver. The first two stages would be the main focus for a pupil panel session, and the second two would be part of what the creative teaching group would do with the data collected.

The discovery stage should take the form of one-to-one interviews between pupils, perhaps from different year groups. The purpose here is to find out exactly what pupils think makes the school tick. What is at the heart of this community? What is its 'positive core'? Give them pre-prepared open-ended questions such as the ones below:

- Think of, and describe, a peak experience or 'high point' in your work or experience at this school that you feel was really creative/exciting/memorable.

- Think about the core factors that give 'life' to this school; the really positive values it can build upon.

- What three wishes would you make to improve further those things that you think are already good about learning and school life?

The dream stage is where pupils form groups that represent a cross-section of the school community. Working together, ideally having collected even more information from their tutor groups or similar, they are encouraged to imagine the future of the school. The gist of the questions they should ask themselves are 'what if ... ?'. This might be drawn from the discovery stage, or might be pre-prepared, such as 'what would the school be like if it was more creative?' They should work together to much as much flesh on their vision as possible, and then present it back to the other groups.

The design stage is where ideas from the discovery and dream stages are 'picked up' by individuals or groups to be explored and developed further. This is then fed back to the whole group. And the delivery stage is simply where the results of the dreaming and designing are applied and followed up. There are several good books on Appreciative Enquiry out there that, if you are interested in this model for organisational change, would be worth reading.

Rapport. What are pupil-staff relations like? Is it easy or difficult for them to get along? Do pupils value and respect feedback from their peers? Are pupils and staff recognized for their achievements? How positive are home-school relations? How do you currently deal with pupils or staff who create barriers to a good level of rapport within the school?

One of the strengths of any school is the variety of people who work there. Hopefully you find that the overall balance of desirable and less desirable qualities that the school's teaching staff possesses creates a happy equilibrium in terms of pupils' overall experience of school life. When encouraging a more creative atmosphere in your school, there will always be members of staff who will be less than supportive, or stuck in their ways. But you must always come back to the question of whether the overall balance is right. I line-managed an excellent teacher who has superb rapport with his pupils, but kept to a rather teacher-centred lesson delivery. When I suggested to him that he might try some more creative methods that were a bit more pupil-centred, he bashfully explained that he rather liked the talking. We arranged a lesson observation where he would attempt to employ a more pupil-centred element to his lesson, which he admitted to enjoying despite the fact that it didn't quite work out right, but what struck me was that he had the most excellent rapport with his class. Not only did he know all their names, which is something that can never be undervalued, he knew their characters and was on excellent terms with them. If you refer back to my lists on pages 85–87 about being valued, and how to nurture that level of rapport, you'll see what I mean. The important thing here is to consider the strengths of your staff – perhaps do a character strengths survey with them as part of an INSET day, see page 47 – and ensure that you have a strong, committed quorum that supports your efforts. Establishing a teaching and learning committee (or community, or better still 'teacher learning communities', a term I prefer in this instance) would be a good way to foster this groundswelling of creative teaching. The effects would trickle down to other teachers as part of the norming to performing levels.

As for rewarding achievements, how well do assemblies get used for this purpose? How well are pupils' achievements kept track of by your pastoral teams? And for staff, do you use staff briefings to celebrate achievements made by staff either within their classrooms or outwith them? I've even seen one school where they have a star teacher noticeboard where pupils give teachers giant gold stars for particularly creative work or lessons. It was done through the pupil council, so it represented a full cross-section of the school, and it became an excellent celebration of the dynamism of staff and a superb awareness tool for other teachers and visitors to the school.

How the school deals with the outside world is equally important. Do you use something like ParentMail to keep your parents and carers regularly informed? How well does your newsletter inspire people about life at the school? What kind of messages does it send out about the ethos of the school? What procedures have you got in place to handle difficult parents, or difficult issues with parents? Is there someone particularly diplomatic and constructive who can help diffuse and resolve situations positively and creatively?

Examples of relevant values and vocabulary that could become mainstream in a creative school: pupil-centred, strengths, celebration, creativity, community (or TLC – teacher learning community).

Structure. What expectations are clearly in place for pupil behaviour, and teacher behaviour, in the classroom? How are these expectations communicated? How willing are pupils and teachers to conform to those expectations? What expectations are there for teachers and support staff in terms of lesson structure, style and content? To what degree are all stakeholders in the school held accountable? How is independent learning encouraged? How are the necessary skill sets taught to pupils?

When a student is able to take control over, and personal responsibility for, their own learning they have developed an important life skill. It is a skill that they will need in the workplace, because many jobs in today's world require an ability to learn new skills and information. And it is a skill that will lead to academic success; when a student discovers things themselves, they will understand the topic with more depth and clarity. But in order for teachers to facilitate this sort of learning, there needs to be consistency across the school when it comes to discipline. Teachers need to use clear, fair and consistent discipline in their classrooms, backed up by an equally clear, fair and consistent school-wide behaviour policy. When this happens even the 'weakest' of teachers can maintain an effective environment for learning. For example, setting the expectation that there should be tripartite lessons taking place in the majority of instances, or that pupils should stand for the teacher and the start and end of lessons (old fashioned, I know, but very effective for establishing a clear beginning and end to the learning) are excellent examples of sound structure.

Discipline, obviously, should not be something oppressive. It should be entirely in the positive. Sometimes, indeed, you need to save pupils from themselves and corrective procedures need to be in place and well communicated to pupils, teachers and parents. But for the majority of pupils in the majority of schools, I feel things can be phrased in the positive. How about talking about a 'can do, will do approach' to your pupils? One where concepts like enterprise and creativity underpin collaboration at all levels to bring about solutions. What about talking of high aspirations and the potential to succeed? Be inclusive and say that doesn't just mean in exams, it means at whatever projects you set your mind to, your school will celebrate that success with you. Have rules, but also have pupil-orientated values in the foreground and ensure that the rules reflect the values.

So talk about showing respect to people, having pride in the school, valuing the support that staff and peers can share; talk about promoting positive behaviour, having high expectations and recognizing and rewarding success; talk about forming strong school–home partnerships to help pupils achieve their potential. Couch everything that affects the majority in fully positive and inclusive language.

> *Examples of relevant values and vocabulary that could become mainstream in a creative school: high expectations, celebrating success, consistency, 'can do, will do', enterprise, collaboration, potential, pride.*

Creativity. What whole-school, cross-curricular and co-curricular events promote creativity? In what ways are pupils encouraged to be enterprising, collaborative, imaginative, resourceful, resilient and autonomous? In what ways are they inspired? In what ways are staff excellent examples of creativity? How well are your creative arts departments integrated with the rest of the school?

Creativity unlocks so much. It develops a pupil's passion for a subject, pupils' enjoyment of a lesson, it rejuvenates teachers, inspires confidence and unlocks potential. Obviously everything in this book is about creativity, so I won't go on about it too much here. But everything that pupils experience needs to radiate creativity. How can your assemblies be improved (more on this later)? How can the displays be more creative? How can *you* be more creative? The basis for creativity across the school is the same as in your classroom. Pupils need to know how to learn, and suitable attempts need to be made to engage with their RAS and their multiple intelligences to stimulate a positive attitude towards learning. Their emotional intelligence will be developed; and they will feel safe, welcomed and valued.

> *Examples of relevant values and vocabulary that could become mainstream in a creative school: imagination, resourcefulness, unlocking potential, inspiring confidence.*

Success criteria. To what degree does the school encourage pupils to improve rather than prove themselves? To what extent do teachers focus on individual progress and not on comparison between pupils? How effective is target-setting and reporting? How well to pupils understand why they did not succeed at something? How well do pupils understand what it is they need to do to improve? Does everyone know what their goals are? What does it look like when pupils flourish?

If you are going to take people on a journey, they need to know where they are going. The school's vision statement needs to be that end point, that success criterion. It needs to give everyone something to aim for, something to become.

Success criteria – or learning objectives by another name – should be part of the everyday life in a creative school. Lessons should have (normally) explicit success criteria, and pupils should have a clear concept of the progress they must make to reach the goals they have set. At an organisational level, teachers need to understand the philosophy of success criteria and utilize them as part of their tripartite lessons and when setting assessments and/or written work. Pastoral care needs to focus on establishing achievable and relevant goals for every pupil, and reviewing those goals against your reporting system. Reports during the year need to reflect real progress and attitude to learning, rather than be summative and in isolation from other reports. When reports come out, tutors need to spend time with each of their pupils reviewing their progress, celebrating successes and planning improvements. Ultimately, you want to foster growth mindsets – a sense that every pupil has success criteria that they can meet.

> *Examples of relevant values and vocabulary that could become mainstream in a creative school: flourish, goals, targets, success criteria, progress, attitude to learning, growth mindsets.*

Learning (independent learning, personalized learning, AfL and study skills). There is a lot in this book about learning. Good, creative learning practices are not all that complicated – they are centred on the concept that pupils should be encouraged to be responsible for, and engaged with, their learning. There are a lot of terms out there to describe the various aspects of the learning process. However, how you go about making this happen is another question. Education in creative study-skills is the initial reaction of many schools. They get a study-skills company in for the day, the pupils learn about how to learn and have a great time. In fact at least one-third of UK secondary schools do this, as that is how many Learning Performance visited in 2010/11. Of course, the impact of visiting experts presenting to your pupils, and to your staff, cannot be underestimated. Anything that stands out will engage with people's RAS, and collapsing the curriculum and having fun and entertaining people in for the day will certainly do that. Any good study-skills day will have taught the pupils a range of skills, and most importantly that learning is not something that happens to them, it is something they make happen. But such an event is most effective when it is part of a school's wider effort to enhance pupils' learning performance and learning experience.

So the next step is a series of lessons on *learning to learn* in PSHE, or some other similar subject. Again, this is good because it gives pupils the ability to put more strategies to the test and find out more about how they learn. Self-reflection can be encouraged and a more mature approach to learning can be developed. They will know from their study-skills day that learning is something they must involve themselves in, and from a good *learning to learn* course they will get a far better opportunity to work out how to get involved.

However, this is not much use if it is something studied in isolation. The rest of their school experience must live up to the strategies and ideals taught. It is no use to pupils if you tell them that they should summarize their units and make maps of them if teachers give them no opportunity to make maps. Pupils are not going to have much luck fostering their own creativity if they do not get opportunities to be creative in their classes. In fact, the best *learning to learn* courses in school are not limited to PSHE, nor are they limited to pupils. Teachers must know and accept these creative learning techniques. They are nothing new, they are not fads; they are tried and tested ideas that are founded on strong educational theory. Realistically, you cannot convince all teachers of the merits of creativity as outlined in this book, but many teachers today are on the side of the ethos of these teaching and learning ideas and would appreciate a co-ordinated whole-school approach.

The first step would be to have an INSET on learning, training them in the kind of information in this book if necessary, and discussing the approaches your school will adopt. You could get teachers to create displays around the school on the different learning styles, or with motivational quotes about learning. Better still, you could get departments to review a scheme of work to see how to improve it by incorporating some creative teaching and assessment for learning into it. Such a day should be both motivational and full of strong educational substance and opportunity – not fluff, nor so many items that no quality time is spent on any one thing.

As well as this, the *learning to learn* lessons should extend across the curriculum. For instance, if multiple intelligences were examined in the relevant subjects, pupils would gain an idea of their strengths and weaknesses in each area. It would also help teachers to appreciate each pupil's learning needs more effectively. You might also want to consider introducing Independent Study, about which there are more details in the next chapter.

Additionally, I think the same teachers should work with the same pupils as often as possible. This allows a decent and effective rapport to be formed where a pupil has a much better chance of receiving a personalized and relevant education as the teacher properly understands the best way to teach each of his or her pupils. I appreciate the downsides from both the administration point of view and the situation where a teacher might be tormented by a relentless bully of a pupil, but in such a situation the good creative school will have effective measures in place to deal with this child's particular issues. 'Time Out' zones, counselling and one-to-one tutoring by a senior member of staff are all examples of an effective approach.

I would also suggest that a creative school form a learning profile for each pupil. Perhaps a page on the school's data management system would be sufficient. It should summarize any learning difficulties the child has, plus results from a VAK test, findings from MI tests, the VIA survey, observations from their form tutor and other key staff about what the pupil is good at doing (negatives would be unnecessary), plus comments from the pupil themselves about what they like doing at school, what their goals are, and so on. Whenever a teacher taught a class, or a pupil, for the first time, they would see this profile which outlined all the good and useful things about a pupil. It might help teachers form a more personalized approach, especially when dealing with a pupil who has not managed to meet the success criteria first time around.

> *Examples of relevant values and vocabulary that could become mainstream in a creative school: learning profile, learning to learn, learning performance, independent study, responsibility, independence, RAS, study skills day, AfL.*

The Creative State. To what extent are teachers aware of, and in control of, their behaviour in the classroom? In the staff room, is there a positive attitude towards the school and its pupils? Do teachers feel inspired to take the initiative and try new things? Do teachers look forward to teaching their lessons? Are teachers engaged in a range of co-curricular activities such as clubs, sport and music? Do staff briefings and CPD motivate staff and instigate creative and tangible outcomes?

Earlier in this book I talked about the importance of entering a creative state when teaching. I think we all recognize the importance and idealism of leaving your stresses at the classroom door, being the best version of yourself and being calm and motivating. So, is this the culture among the staff in your school? A ex-colleague of mine recently commented that on the first day back after the summer break in her new school, the comment she heard most among the staff was 'well, that's one day less to go'. It's really important, if any of the ideas in this book are to come to fruition in any extensive way in your school, to have a zest for learning and teaching among the staff. Again, this could be a focus point of your creative teaching community: what is it that this school has to celebrate? By concentrating on what is right with the school, and using that as a platform to make positive changes, there will ultimately be a new energy among staff, pupils and parents alike. It's vital that teachers feel empowered to teach, rather than simply discipline or, worse, feel like zoo-keepers, so discipline and a fresh start in September may well be the first steps to encouraging more staff to enter their creative states.

> Examples of relevant values and vocabulary that could become mainstream in a creative school: creative state, zest for learning, fresh start.

3.3 Building the Creative School

Vision and Values

From the process in the previous chapter, you may well have quite a few ideas that are applicable directly to your school. As I said before, I am not going to be prescriptive. But to be illustrative, here's a diagram of the six values I would promote and foster as a creative school. The first three are statements 'from' the school – values that the school will do their best to foster. The second three are 'from' the pupil – values that they would ideally try to develop in themselves, and values that the school would help them advance in.

As for the vision statement, would that work in your school? My school's vision statement is 'A leading creative community; an enduring love of learning.' And my sixth form's vision statement is: 'Sixth Formers are accomplished in their specialisms and passionate about their future; they flourish in the pursuit of excellence.' Both of these statements try to paint a picture of what the school is ideally like. It gives staff and pupils an aspiration. And it works. A quick search online for other schools' vision statements will tell you that there is a lot of variety, with some being rather vague or bland, and others being very clear and accessible.

Whatever you and your team decide, the vision statement and associated values should be displayed in all literature. The vision statement should appear on letterheads, the prospectus, forms, internal documents, the website, the virtual learning platform, handouts to pupils, classroom walls, corridor noticeboards and so on. The associated values should be prominently displayed around the school, in the prospectus and on the website. The vision statement and associated values must be fleshed out and explained, so that everyone is clear on exactly what the success criteria is. So for example:

- *A creative zest for learning and life.* We aim to provide outstanding and motivating opportunities for all our pupils to really enjoy learning, to be part of the learning process and to establish the skills needed to enjoy and flourish in their life beyond school.

- *Learning is a skill for life.* Knowing how you learn, and taking personal responsibility for your learning as a result, is a really important life skill. You will always need to learn new things as you grow older: in the workplace, as you form relationships with people, as you become parents, as you grow more aware of the world around you. So we want to help you become independent learners.

- *Everyone is valued, everyone is nurtured.* No one size fits all. We want to know each and every pupil: their needs, their characters and their hopes. We want to help you form your goals and learn who you are. We want everyone to work together creatively towards their futures and support each other as each pupil unlocks their potential.

- *Personal success and wellbeing are important.* We want to celebrate your successes, both in the classroom and outside the classroom. It is important to manage your emotional wellbeing so that you can focus on your studies and your aspirations with clarity of mind. We want to help you be resilient, healthy and happy in yourself.

- *I aim for a 'Can Do, Will Do' attitude.* We want for you to develop a growth mindset where you are ambitious about what you can do, now and in your future. We want you to be enterprising and collaborative. Teachers will do their best to be creative in their lessons, and we will see a high number of you participating in the classroom and in a range of activities outside the classroom too.

- *I have pride and respect for my school's community.* We are all proud to be part of our school's community. We will all look after the building and each other. We all feel an affinity for its ability to inspire confidence and help us form our futures. We understand that we all have a responsibility to challenge anything that undermines what we stand for. We will celebrate each other's strengths and successes together, and respect each other's feelings and identities so that everyone can feel happy, safe and can achieve their potential.

- *I aspire towards responsibility for my learning and my life.* We will all have high expectations of what you can achieve now and in the future. You will have a positive attitude towards your learning, as you take control of how you learn and how you behave. You will work together with your teachers and your peers to set targets for your future, and you will always be aware of how you can improve your learning performance and ultimately flourish as a happy and successful person.

I hope that the above is a useful starting point for you and your school. I've tried to incorporate the vocabulary from this chapter but there may well be other values and vocabulary that would be more relevant to your school's circumstances. I would display the vision and values around the school, as an A4 poster in all the classrooms and as bigger posters around the rest of the school. I would run an assembly on each area, starting with the vision statement and then going through each value. You could get different form classes to do each assembly to get their take on it.

Let's turn our attention to what this vision, its associated values and vocabulary would look like both in and out of the classroom.

In the Classroom

Displays. The school's vision statement and values should be prominently displayed in every classroom in the school. Teachers could refer to it as part of their positive behaviour management strategies. You might like to consider a universal 'rules of the classroom' poster too, to create some uniformity and clarity of expectation. Rules that come from the values could be:

- enter the classroom quietly, in an orderly manner and ready to learn

- stand at the start and end of the lesson and wait for the teacher's instructions

- show respect towards everyone in the classroom and keep focussed on the learning

- participate in the learning as actively as you can

- follow the teacher's instructions carefully

- reflect on what knowledge and skills you learned or developed in this lesson

I also suggest that you produce an A4 poster listing the top features of a creative lesson for all teachers to display near their desks. Things to include would be:

- the lesson followed the three-part structure

- success criteria were shared with the pupils at the start of the lesson and reflected upon at the end of the lesson

- pupils were aware of where they were in the unit, connections were made with previous and future lessons, and opportunities were given to pupils to review their learning and develop their study skills.

- there was assessment for learning in the lesson

- opportunities were made to encourage independent learning skills

- subject-specific skills, as well as knowledge, were developed in this lesson

- at least one major aspect of the lesson was distinctively creative: it was designed to connect with pupils' RAS, used VAK and/or MI, and was enjoyed by the majority

- pupils were actively involved with the lesson and their learning

- the lesson was pupil-centred

- you were in your creative state and continued to build a positive rapport with pupils

Observations. Obviously the progress from norming to performing needs to be monitored. Lesson observations are a really important way to make sure that the vision is being followed through. Each school will have its own model for observing teaching, so you will need to consider how best to incorporate the success criteria for creative teaching as outlined in this book into your observation model. I also rather like the star teachers' noticeboard as voted for by pupils, as I mentioned on page 145. This isn't a popularity contest, this is an opportunity for pupils to highlight work they really enjoyed and benefited from in recent lessons. It is also an excellent way to raise awareness of creative teaching across the school.

The Sixth Form. Does everything in this book apply to the sixth form too? Well, yes. But I appreciate that some people might find that a bit difficult; after all we're meant to be getting them ready for university aren't we? So that means there should be lots of lectures and reading, right? Well, there's a definite place for all of that, but the sixth form is a transition time between school and university so you cannot put pupils in at the deep end like that. Just because they've done their GCSEs, some work experience and a bit more growing up doesn't mean they've become adults quite yet. Sixth formers need to be given ways to engage, just the same as any learner at any age. And it is still true that real learning takes place when pupils discover things for themselves, rather than copy down your lecture parrot fashion. So, go on, get creative with your sixth form too.

Out of the Classroom

Most pupils will spend more than one-quarter of their time in school outside of lessons. And I'm not talking about pupils who bunk off. Form/registration time, assemblies, break and lunch times all add up to a considerable amount of time spent out of the classroom.

So what does your school do with its pupils to foster creativity, encourage a good attitude to learning and stimulate their RAS during out-of-classroom time? You might like to write in your thoughts to the questions about form/registration time and assemblies below.

Form Time. What activities have you and your colleagues used in this time to foster creativity and engage pupils effectively, preparing them for learning? What creative and stimulating activities are encouraged or required of tutors in this time, beyond taking the register and reading the notices? Is there a bank of resources for teachers to use? Personally, I prefer the term personal tutoring. The tutor is really there to monitor and encourage the progress of each individual pupil, not the whole group.

Tutors should be approachable, tactful and interested in young people's wellbeing. They should not be there to get pupils into trouble, they should be there to help pupils make reparations and to set targets for future improvement. They are the main link between the school, parents and pupils and so they should be excellent ambassadors for the school – promoting positive learning behaviour through the school's vision and values.

But most of all, they should know the pupils in their tutor group. They should hold regular one-to-one meetings with each member of their group during tutor time. In these one-to-one meetings pupils can discuss their learning performance, set targets for the future and celebrate recent successes. If the pupil has a problem, their tutor should be the first teacher they turn to for help and support.

There should be an extended period of time (20 to 30 minutes) every day during which form time, assemblies and house meetings can take place. This regular opportunity for pupils to meet their tutor, a familiar and positive influence, is a key aspect of successfully fostering a creative school. In addition to one-to-one meetings, tutors could lead on fun, creative quizzes. Even getting pupils to try out quizzes on sporcle.com is excellent for mental stimulation and out-of-the-box thinking. Having an inter-tutor-group competition is even better. Get tutor groups to come up with tricky quizzes and games to challenge each other with, with a prize at the end of the year for a winner. This is a sure-fire community-builder and ties in brilliantly with a zest for learning and life. You could also get tutor groups to teach each other things. Anything useful in life that isn't on the national curriculum, for instance how to tie a tie, how to wrap presents, or how aeroplanes work, and so on. This would encourage enterprise and collaboration.

Beyond this, lunchtime clubs and activities are really helpful in developing and honing creative skills. And organisations such as Young Enterprise, the Wings of Hope, Target 2.0 and the Duke of Edinburgh Scheme all go a long way to cultivate the values discussed in this book.

Assemblies. Tick any of the following that apply.

☐ I don't go to assemblies as they are boring and I can get on with marking instead.

☐ I don't mind going to assemblies.

☐ I don't mind going to assemblies, and sometimes I'll even learn something I didn't know!

- [ ] Assemblies do a lot to motivate pupils for the day, with a good strong focus on things that are relevant to the pupils.

- [ ] A range of staff get involved in running assemblies.

- [ ] Pupils seem to enjoy assemblies.

- [ ] Pupils do not seem to like assemblies.

- [ ] Pupils are passive during assemblies, and in their opinion of assemblies.

- [ ] There is scope for doing more to improve the content of assemblies.

- [ ] There is scope for doing more to improve the conduct of assemblies.

Your responses could be something of an indication of how creative your school is. If teachers and management are bothered enough to attempt to create stimulating assemblies and enjoyable form times, then this will have an impact on the pupils' attitude to the school. Pupils will notice that people are trying to make their time as well-spent as possible, and will (eventually) be appreciative. Moreover, they will be better prepared mentally for learning; they will be more positive and more receptive in class. And these are the principal reasons for encouraging the creative school ethos. It is not solely up to teachers in their classrooms to encourage and enable pupils; if creativity is to be encouraged throughout the school, then there needs to be a team effort from staff at all levels.

Websites such as assemblies.org.uk have a range of easily adaptable, and free, assemblies on a broad range of topics. I suggest that you make assemblies thematic – so that several assemblies in a row are on related topics. This would also be an important vehicle for sharing vision and values.

Independent Study. Independent Study is time spent reviewing and digesting information learned in the school day. It aims to empower pupils to take more control of their learning by giving them a structured daily routine to organize and revise their notes from classes. This helps them to manage their workload and have much better subject knowledge. By feeling more responsible for their studies in this way, pupils will be more actively involved in the learning process and will ultimately become better learners now and in the future. At my school, it has really helped pupils to get into good, independent, study habits for the GCSEs, A-levels and life after school. There are plenty of ways to set this up.

What we do at my school is to require pupils to spend half-an-hour a night reviewing their learning. Pupils are expected to have a folder containing a sheet of paper for each subject topic they are presently studying. Each day pupils simply add on to these sheets what they learned in class. This can be bullet pointed and should contain the main ideas and prompts to aid their recall of various details. It could even be done on a computer if preferred.

Pupils then use the remaining time to review what they have written down on previous days, especially what they wrote yesterday and last week. Pupils are encouraged to be creative with this process and to spend time testing themselves by rewriting notes from memory, giving a talk to an imaginary audience and so on.

Every time they do this they strengthen the neural connections in their brain, improving their memory and removing the need to cram for exams. They will also make better connections with information being learned in class.

We also advise pupils to summarize a recently completed topic of work using both creativity and clear structure, usually in the form of something creative and logical, like a map (see page 78). Independent Study also includes anything else that promotes real learning, such as watching a relevant TV programme, visiting exhibitions or reading articles on the web. Parents could spend five minutes with their child to ask them what they can remember from their independent study session; this will further improve memory. Pupils bring in their independent study notes to school for their form tutors and classmates to compare and discuss, which reinforces yet again what they have learned and promotes peer and independent learning.

The benefits are clear, and I would explain them to pupils like this:

- continually reviewing work keeps it fresh in your mind

- because it is fresh in your mind you will form better connections with new information learned

- this in turn will lead to a better level of understanding

- Independent Study prevents cramming and promotes real learning

- Independent Study will get you better marks

- Independent Study gets you into good study habits for GCSE and A-level

For some subjects, such as maths and languages, Independent Study needs to be more about applying the learning rather than revising the learning, so allow departments to set guidelines as to what ideas and methods suit their subject the best. I should also point out here that the name *independent* study means just that. While it is worth monitoring it and helping pupils get it right at first, ultimately it is the pupils' own study and shouldn't be treated in quite the same way as homework. A survey of parents revealed that about 80 per cent of our pupils did their Independent Study to one degree or another. Even if only 40 per cent did it in your school, that would still be a significant number of pupils who have taken control and responsibility for their learning in their own particular creative style. Add in a few 'celebration days' a few well-timed emails, and some information evenings for pupils, parents and staff, and you have a powerful, personalized, positive learning tool.

School Audit: Maslow's Hierarchy of Needs

There have been lots of ideas and concepts covered in this section, and it is worth taking the opportunity to review your own school. Maslow's Hierarchy of Needs is a well-known tool, and I suggest you use it to analyse how well your school meets pupils' needs and creates the right environment for learning.

Abraham Maslow was born in 1908 in New York. As his parents were uneducated Jewish immigrants, they pushed their son towards academic success. Because of this, as a child, he was quite isolated, spending most of his time with books. He went on to study psychology and gained his PhD in 1934. It is fair to say that his goal was to make psychology relevant, more human, than a whole load of theorizing.

Early in his career Maslow worked with monkeys. It interested him that some needs took precedence over others. For example, if you are hungry and thirsty you tend to quench your thirst first because you can go without food for longer than you can without water. Likewise, if you are extremely thirsty but someone has got you in a headlock and you cannot breathe, which is more important? The need to breathe, of course. So Maslow took this idea and created his well-known hierarchy of needs. Although they are not scientifically tested, they seem to have rung true with most people and there seems to be little for people to disagree with. Here is a diagram of the hierarchy:

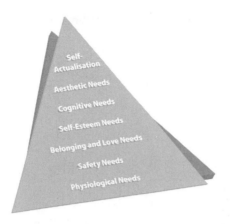

The first four needs – physiological needs, safety, belonging and self-esteem – are deficiency needs. That is to say they are needs that need to be met so that an individual can grow as an individual, represented by the remaining needs.

Physiological needs include things like breathing, hunger, thirst, the right vitamins and nutrients, bodily comforts and so on. Safety needs include the need for structure, feeling secure in your surroundings and having stability in your life. Belonging needs are the needs to be socially accepted and to be loved. Having friends, a sense of community and affectionate relationships are all examples of belonging needs. The last deficiency need is self-esteem needs. There are two levels of self-esteem needs. The lower level is the need for respect from other people, status, recognition, attention, reputation, appreciation and dignity. The higher-level self-esteem need is internal: it is the need for self-respect, self-confidence, achievement, competence, independence and freedom.

If these needs are not met, then future growth is not possible. If you are deficient in one of these needs, then you will seek to fulfil it, and you will not be satisfied until it is met. Once it has been met, though, it will cease to be a source of motivation. When one of these needs is not fulfilled, it can trigger the stress mechanism I referred to earlier in the book, but this time it can be the source of serious neurosis. It might explain why badly behaved children often seem satisfied with their behaviour – it fulfils both belonging and self-esteem needs because they get recognition and a role to play in their community that they may feel they are unable to get by more positive means.

Maslow's growth needs are divided into two levels. The first level contains our cognitive and aesthetic needs. Cognitive needs focus on learning, understanding and exploring. Aesthetic needs are the appreciation of art, order (think especially maths, science and languages) and beauty. Note the left- and right-brain focus of both these needs. They are creative and intellectual, and they are what go on in our classrooms all the time.

The higher level of growth need is self-actualization. This one is a lot less clearly defined than the other levels. It is different because once found, these needs continue to motivate and be felt. It is basically when you realize your potential. It has also been suggested that self-transcendence, when you help other people find self-fulfilment and realize their potential, should be added to the top of the hierarchy.

It is worth pointing out that few people achieve complete self-actualization; so what about the rest? A creative school will be one that seeks to provide the best possible opportunities for pupils, and staff, to explore and improve their abilities – to grow and flourish. And to do so it must make sure that, where it can, it caters for all levels of needs. You can hardly expect a pupil to learn (cognitive needs) if he or she is lacking in the first four needs.

Physiological needs: some ideas

- breakfast club
- healthy food in the canteen
- water in the classrooms
- parents' cookery classes
- classroom check

The physiological need is not just to provide food and drinks, but to provide the right sustenance. While we know that a healthy, balanced diet is easy to provide, getting pupils to eat it is another matter. Moreover, it there seems to be uncertainty about whether or not fizzy drinks and chocolate are good or bad for pupils because tests regularly demonstrate different findings! With the government's recent directives about the kind of food that must be served in schools, it looks like schools will now start to meet the healthy food need. Something of a school project could ensue from this. Not only could pupils learn about what's good and bad for them, but you could also combine the activity with an enterprise project to promote imaginary brands of healthy food.

But what about your tuck shop? Now there isn't a lot to stop pupils buying their own supply of sweets and chocolate from the newsagent down the road, so there is little point in the ban on selling chocolates in your school. Not that chocolate is particularly bad for most pupils. While too much chocolate is definitely bad for health and brainpower, research suggests that a little bit of chocolate can give pupils a bit of a boost when it comes to mental energy. However, you should ensure that an adequate supply of fruit, smoothies and cereal bars are also for sale because these are definitely good for health and brainpower. Moreover, the sale of fair trade goods will help to meet a social affiliation/belonging need.

While food and drink are primary physiological needs that schools can meet with some reasonably straightforward innovation, there are other needs too. The physical environment within the classroom and around the school can cover many needs (for instance, an aesthetic need), but most basically if it is too hot, too stuffy, too cramped, too dark or too cold, then pupils' focus will rightly be on their discomfort rather than on your lesson. While a teacher can be responsible for a good room layout and keeping it tidy and well-ordered, more fundamental issues are obviously a school management responsibility. There is a classroom evaluation form in the previous section of this book; perhaps this could be distributed to all staff to assess needs across the school.

Safety needs: some ideas

- anti-bullying campaigns
- friendly atmosphere/ethos
- non-threatening teaching staff/positive behaviour management
- vertical forms
- pupil mentoring/buddying scheme

While a school cannot do very much about a pupil's home life, I would say it was a prerequisite of any successful school to provide a safe, stable environment for its pupils. How can you expect pupils to concentrate on learning if they feel threatened by people in the classes? Or if they are more interested in threatening their classmates because there is little to convince them in the structure and ethos of the school that bad behaviour is less enjoyable than good behaviour?

This is a complex issue that goes well beyond the scope of this book. Suffice it to say that if this is a problem in your school, then action on it must come from senior management. There need to be pupil-led campaigns in which they learn about creating a happy community. There need to be teacher action groups to review, develop and implement plans to improve ethos and behaviour – again, there's the *Happy, Safe and Achieving Potential* questionnaire available on the companion website. But most of all the initiatives need to come from the top, with the head leading assemblies and being proactive on the issue.

Belonging needs: some ideas

- pupils and staff feeling valued and appreciated
- anti-bullying
- clubs and societies
- sports and music
- proactive attempt to be inclusive
- inter-tutor-group competitions
- house system

If a school is to be creative, then it needs to practise what it preaches. And the best way to demonstrate creativity is to provide a range of opportunities for pupils. Most schools have clubs and interest groups, but how many and of what quality? This is an ideal opportunity to bring in multiple intelligences. Can you group all the clubs, groups and annual activities into the eight multiple intelligences? Are there any intelligences that could be better represented? If not, then give your school an imaginary pat on the back. If there are gaps, then here is a chance to make a real difference and enhance the feeling of belonging, and most likely self-esteem, needs of more pupils than you do already.

On the same note, what about your school's staff? Do they feel valued and part of the community, or are they more isolated? How well do they socialize, in and out of the staff room? How cliquey are they? The way in which senior management deals with the school's staff is very important: not being too detached or abrupt, remembering to smile and say hello, joining them at break time, and so on. It tends to be the little things that make people happy, so things like this can make a big difference. If staff are happier, then their approach to problems will be more positive and they will have a more positive impact on pupils' attitudes as well. If teachers are role models for pupils, then it should be borne in mind that senior management are role models for teachers.

Self-esteem needs: some ideas

- display area for work
- school has knowledge of pupils' strengths and acts accordingly
- positive criticism
- merit system
- active recognition for good work/behaviour
- removal of unnecessary negative language
- rapid feedback of work
- use of study skills

This is such a wide-ranging area of school life. Adults can often trace their insecurities about their competence in certain areas to the way that they were discouraged or encouraged at school. Personally, I was never very good at Craft, Design and Technology at school. While I was good at designing (my work received a lot of praise), my ability to make anything in the workshop was barely adequate. It was never terrible, I never managed to hurt myself or anyone else and the end product was recognizable and functional. In fact I tended to try very hard to get it right. But my CDT teacher never really gave me much encouragement; in fact he usually just frowned at my efforts. So halfway through that GCSE I gave up and transferred to another GCSE.

It was fortunate that my school was supportive and helped me storm through a different GCSE, but even today I look upon things from Ikea with suspicion! I usually give DIY work to someone else to do for fear of messing it up. Don't get me wrong, I don't blame my CDT teacher for my dislike of home maintenance; today I am quite capable of making my own decisions and attempts on these things. But my confidence, and possibly abilities, might be greater when doing so if he had been a little more supportive and encouraging. Teenage minds are very open to your feedback, both positive and negative, and it is important that we build people up rather than bring them down.

A lot of the bullet points above follow on from the contents of this book and need no other explanation. A few do though. The removal of unnecessary negative language refers to things like signs that say 'Do not run in the corridor', which can seem rather authoritarian and therefore something to be derided or a rule to be broken. I suggest it becomes 'For safety reasons, walk in the corridor, please'.

It is worth mentioning merit systems and other ways to recognize achievements. First there must be a system to recognize achievement in your school. For instance, if there are slips of paper to complain about poor work, there must also be slips of paper to commend good work. If there is a merit system, it must be easy to add points for good work. Is there a display board in departments or in prominent places around the school to put up good work? Ask pupils to assess themselves more often – get them to identify two things they think they did well in their work and maybe one thing they think they could do better, then give them feedback focused on how much you agree with the points they identified. And then highlight what else they did well too.

It can be a good idea to have a house system too. Many schools abandoned these because they thought they were divisive, but I disagree. They can aid safety, belonging and esteem needs through fun inter-house competitions (think talent shows and sports day as well as maths challenge days, entrepreneurship and other subject-based competitions), and vertical forms where pupils are grouped by house and not by age – this then enables a good mentoring system between older and younger pupils.

Cognitive needs: some ideas

- students know how to learn
- use of study skills
- use of AfL
- use of VAK and multiple intelligences in teaching
- stillness and wellbeing
- regular revision built into the timetable/curriculum
- knowledge of students' preferred learning styles
- pupil-centred approach to teaching and learning
- opportunities to get involved with subject material and the learning process

The use of mindfulness, or stillness, in schools is an interesting area of recent development. Getting pupils to sit in a meditative atmosphere before the start of school is one example of mindfulness in action. And so is encouraging pupils to be aware of, and in control of, their thoughts. In order for pupils to be able to explore, learn and understand, they need to explore, learn and understand who they are too. As the words inscribed on the Temple at Delphi in Ancient Greece once said: 'know thyself'. That ancient wisdom is still relevant today and as we have seen earlier, the creative school has to help pupils discover themselves. Hampton and Tonbridge Schools have been particularly proactive in this area. Search online for 'mindfulness in schools' to find out more.

These ideas to meet cognitive needs are exemplified throughout the book. Hopefully it has become clear by now that things really work best when they are not deployed by teachers in isolation from each other. A school-wide approach that motivates and enables pupils and staff to do these things is the best way to encourage creativity and academic success. In other words successfully creative schools establish a creative vision, values and vocabulary, have study-skills days, have courses built in across the curriculum to build on these learning skills, give teachers time to work as a department on developing exciting new lessons, make sure that pupils build a continuous review of their work into their homework schedules, make sure that the food on offer is suitable and make sure that everything that can be done is being done to ensure pupils and staff enjoy being at school. Ultimately you will find that pupils will be ready and more able to think creatively, improve their learning performance and develop that creative zest for learning and life.

3.4 Conclusion

Everyone is creative and everyone has their own creative style, whether they realize it yet or not. Tests to measure your preferred learning style, multiple intelligences, character strengths, emotional intelligence and so forth are ways to help you access your creativity. In reality you can never pigeonhole a person into wholly being a 'visual learner' or being dominated by an 'aesthetic intelligence'. So when working with pupils, it is important for them to have ownership over their creative style and to be responsible for employing their creativity in their learning.

For the teacher's part, they need to provide a range of opportunities across their lessons for pupils to put their creativity into action. This means being inventive and pupil-centred, facilitating the learning. It does not mean doing it for them, or spending hours preparing lots of creative resources. It means creating a safe, welcoming atmosphere, building a good rapport with their pupils and creating enjoyable learning activities.

From a whole-school perspective, facilitating creativity means to create the right ethos and environment for creativity to thrive. It needs to be a happy and safe place for pupils, where their wellbeing is enhanced and they are protected from bullying and indiscipline. It is a place where learning and achievement is seen as something that is for everyone. Creativity is stimulated from all angles: a vision statement, associated values, common vocabulary, displays, letterheads, home–school communication, the website, the VLE, the dining hall, form time, assembly, clubs, activities, off-curriculum days, and of course, lessons. We should all be able to learn with style, and I hope the ideas in this book can help you achieve just that.

I'm really keen to hear how you've got on, and if you have any creative ideas that you would like to share, please get in touch with me: david@learningperformance.com.

Bibliography

Assessment Reform Group (Broadfoot et al) (2002), *Assessment for Learning: 10 Principles*, www.assessment-reform-group. org.uk.

Bandler, R., Grinder, J. *et al.* (1981), *Frogs into Princes: Neuro-Linguistic Programming*, Moab, UT: Real People Press.

Campaign for Learning (2010), www.campaign-for-learning.org. uk/cfl/learninginschools/projects/learningtolearn/learning_ to_learn_project_findings.asp.

Claxton, Guy (2002), *Building Learning Power: Helping Young People Become Better Learners*, Bristol: TLO.

Cowley, Sue (2011), *Getting the Buggers to Behave*, fourth edition. London: Continuum.

Dweck, Carol (2006), *Mindset: The New Psychology of Success*, New York: Random House.

Gardner, H. (1999), *Intelligence Reframed: Multiple Intelligences for the 21st Century*, New York: Basic Books.

Gilbert, Christine (2007) in *Teaching and Learning in 2020 Review,* nsonline.org.uk/node/83151.

Goleman, Daniel (1996), *Emotional Intelligence: Why it Can Matter More Than IQ*, London: Bloomsbury.

Kline, P. (1997) *The Everyday Genius: Restoring Children's Natural Joy of Learning, and Yours Too*, Salt Lake City, UT: Great River Books.

Mayer, J. D., Salovey, P. & Brackett, M. A. (2004), *Emotional Intelligence: Key Readings on the Mayer and Salovey Model*, New York: DUDE Publishing.

Seligman, Martin (2011), *Flourish: A New Understanding of Happiness and Well-Being – and How To Achieve Them*, London: Nicholas Brealey Publishing.

Specific Diagnostic Studies Inc. (1999), www.thelearningweb.net/chapter03/page130.html.

Tuckman, B (1965), 'Developmental Sequence in Small Groups' *Psychological Bulletin* 63, pp. 384–399.

University of Pennsylvania (2007), www.ppc.sas.upenn.edu/index.html.

Index